This book is dedicated to the people of West Africa: those who I have met, those who I have experienced, and those who I have never known. Writing this book has given me many pleasures and sorrows as I remember all that I have witnessed. I thank CreateSpace.com for enabling me to publish this book. Finally, I thank my parents for all of their help and wonderful support.

-August Kelly   June 2010

Forward

I met August Kelly shortly after his return from West Africa while I was teaching at Santa Barbara City College. Having invited him to speak in my geography classes each semester since then, one thing became apparent: The students were way more into his enthralling descriptions of life in the jungle and his Peace Corps adventures than they were with my scripted lectures. I quickly realized that I had violated an important rule, and advice, of my mentor Wendell Hyde: "Get a good guest speaker, not a great one, so the kids will want you back." Envy could not help but exude from me in the back row as students would stay riveted after class ended in order to hear the fate of "Mr. Rooster," or how August became "Snake Proof."

Obsessed with the notion that these stories needed to be shared in a broader context, I was elated to receive a copy of the JuJu Chronicles.

In reading the JuJu Chronicles, I find myself wanting to speed ahead to catch the next sentence, yet the words in front of me hold my attention: I am paced by their cadence. I am torn after each story as whether to re-read the previous story, or hungrily start the next. I now own a book held together by rubber bands, having read each story countless times. What worries and troubles I use to carry, burdens that use to weight me down, are gone. Nothing I have experienced measures or compares to these; however, it is the laughter, joy and love unveiled in the JuJu chronicles that keeps me coming back.

The JuJu Chronicles weave a web of enchantment, terror and adventure. "Malaria and "Hunger" chronicles the real danger and pain the jungle produces. My personal favorite (as August will tell you), has always been "Mr. Rooster." "Diamonds and Gold" drags you deep into the workings of JuJu and the subtle nature of love. Watch out for genies and leopard-men! Surf West Africa? You bet, with "Wah-Wah Wood." Don't forget to call your local witch doctor if you have extra cash… "Gboyo" reveals the genocide and civil war that has engulfed Liberia (it is not for the faint of heart). The JuJu Chronicles will take you to the edge of your seat, again and again, until you fall off.

Enjoy, Carl Sunbeck

----------------**From the ash we shall rise**----------------
-

May the tears

Of our grief

Water the seeds

We now must plant

And may we reap

From this bitter soil

A brighter bloom

And a sweeter fruit

From which to feast

MALARIA DREAMS

The rhythmic beating of drums pulsed through the dense tropical jungle, protected from above by a canopy of trees extending a hundred feet or more into the sky. They are known as the talking drums and he could feel them talking to him as he lay in the heat, his mind blanketed in the sweltering humidity, his feverish body soaked in sweat. A swarm of mosquitoes danced about the room seeking his body, seeking his blood to feast upon, leaving behind a parasite as a reminder of their presence, leaving him with malaria and its delirium. Don felt this in his mind, something real but not real. Everything here in West Africa is like these, like the rhythmic beating of drums.

Like his dreams, his mind ached from the pain in his bones. The first signs of a malaria attack are the shivers. How odd to be so cold when it's so hot outside, having to wrap oneself in blankets while others fanned their half naked bodies in a futile attempt to ease themselves from the tropical jungle heat. It was as though the marrow of his bones was slowly turning into ice, it was as if he was being frozen solid from the inside out; then the fever strikes, melting the frozen marrow into lava: A fever borne from the larvae erupting to life within Don's internal organs, larvae deposited there by the mosquitoes' bite, larvae dancing on the jungle's rhythm culminating in a mind breaking fever where all is ultimately lost, except the beating of drums and the pain of sleeping on rocks.

Sweat from his forehead fell into his eyes blurring his vision and any sense of reality his mind may still have held. He could no longer distinguish that from which his eyes told him and that from which his mind told him: Both were miserable and painful. The floor beneath him appeared to be undulating like a gentle rolling sea and the full moon that filtered through his open window cast strange silvery shadows upon those exact waters. Don, rubbing his eyes, forced himself to concentrate on the floor. It wasn't the floor that was moving but something that was moving on the floor, something that was twisting and slithering about. And it wasn't one thing, but many things, hundreds of things, thousands of things weaving and intertwining within themselves, a multitude of unknown creatures emitting horrible guttural hissing sounds of aggravation and warning.

Don diverted his attention away from the floor in an attempt to curl himself into a ball, but the rocks he imagined he slept upon kept bruising his body and the more he tried to relieve the pain, the more the burden grew. The rhythmic cadence of beating drums born deep within the jungle's womb grew louder and louder, feeding his delirium. Don, tossing and turning, was caught once again by the full moon's spell casting shadows of elongated patterns which carpeted the floor beneath him, shadows of shimmering diamonds outlined in black and white borders, shadows of fat limbless bodies crawling about, shadows inhabiting and filling every corner.

Struggling to force his mind away from the mass at the foot of his bed, he refocused his attention outside towards the flames of a bonfire, flames exposing silhouetted figures that hurriedly moved about anxiously adding wood to a towering fire causing embers and sparks to fly high into the night. He watched the embers ride up towards the moon as they spread out into the airless darkness; and he watched them as they fell into his room, settling down like a light burning snow, a snow that landed upon the checkered backs of the shadowy squirming creatures, causing them to strike and lash out at one another.

The increasing pace of beating drums pulled his mind back to the fire where he witnessed people dancing to the various rhythms they produced, each limb catching a different beat; and as the flames grew higher, they too danced higher, dancing and jumping to the synchronized sound of crackling flames and embers.

Singing voices flooded Don's ears as well as the jungle, singing voices that called out to someone or some thing that lived somewhere in the jungle, somewhere between the shadows dividing the past from the future; voices that sang out to an unknown being lurking in the swamps and the undergrowth, a creature that was neither man nor animal. His mind pounded from the images conjured up by the drums, images of a place he knew little about, a place he now called home, a place where each day he knew less and less about, and under the spell of malaria, a place in which he knew nothing, nothing of what he heard or saw. Yet, still he saw, he saw floating on their beckoning voices a wooden face streaked with horizontal lines spiked by two large spiraling horns protruding from a blackened chiseled skull carrying a pair of burning red eyes: He saw before him, dancing on the rhythm of their hypnotic beat, the country devil.

The rhythmic beat of the talking drums drew closer and closer, and as Don struggled to stop the torment of his delirium, the snakes twisting about the floor pulled themselves tighter and tighter until they had successfully entangled themselves into a giant knot; whereupon, they set themselves out to swallowing and devouring one another under the gentle falling burning snow.

Outside, by the fiery flames, frantic dancers moved faster and faster, bending lower and lower and jumping higher and higher while singing voices rose louder and louder; until finally, the country devil himself, stood in the middle of the flames with outstretched arms speaking words that stood above all other noises: Words that burned themselves into Don's brain, branding him forever. Then all was black, except for the smoldering glow of embers and ash.

From the silence of the coals came the laughter, and from the laughter came a smiling image, the smiling image of Sompon Weah. Sompon, all twelve years of him, was reading a book, reading with enthusiasm and pride: Smiling, laughing and reading. Don remembered the first time he meet Sompon. Sompon would pass by Don's hut each morning on his way to the river where he would fish and bathe. Don, being new to the village, was required to set out on a table a pan of kola nut, some salt and grounded red

pepper as an offering and an invitation to his neighbors.
He also had to buy "the something." "The something"
was local distilled rum.

One day, Sompon decided he would take the jar
of pepper that Don had set aside on the table. When
Don caught him stealing the jar, he picked Sompon up
and told him he was going to carry him into the brush
and chop him up and eat him. And as Sompon started
kicking and screaming, Don told the crying boy, if he
ever stole from him again, he would do exactly as he
said; however, if he ever needed anything, anything at
all, all he needed to do was ask him. So the very strange
relationship began.

Deep within the coals sat a figure; a figure gently
swinging in a hammock under a giant almond tree
whose broad leaves and wide branches offered shade

and comfort to the many people who walked past. Faka was picking at a hand made guitar and singing songs in a very high-pitched voice, songs that Don did not understand. Faka's teenage friends sat around him listening intently, clapping and praising Faka after each and every song. Faka was smiling, a smile filled with pride and joy, a smile matched only by Sompon Weah's laughter.

Chea Dee stood naked in the rekindling fire, her hands held down by her waist, her deep brown skin glowing in the coals amber hue. She slowly opened her eyes, her thick dark eyelashes unveiling more lightness than all the stars in the darkest and clearest of nights. She, like all the women here, knew all the dances that African girls learned as children. She reached out from the coals pressing her burning flesh against his tanned white skin while moving her hands through his long smooth hair as he gently pulled on her braided locks. He felt her strong young slender body on his sweat soaked skin. Her touch was soft and always present, like her smile. Slowly they walked to the river's edge and swam to the center of the stream under a "deep-less" night filled with the burning embers of diamonds.

A shotgun blast reverberated throughout the village. Don saw the bright red-hot blast that killed the woman and saw Sompon holding the other end, tears streaming down his face. The headless woman, who gathered his tears, was the eldest wife of all of his father's wives. Months earlier, she had grown insanely jealous and bitter of Sompon's mother and had her sent away. It was while his mother was away that she was swept from the rocks and drowned. Rumors had spread through the village that the eldest wife had placed JuJu on Sompon's mother, allowing the genies to grab her, allowing them to pull her into the river, allowing them to drown her. This is how Don came to know Sompon.

The three-room mud hut they called a jail was no more than a hundred yards from Don's own hut. Don had gone to the authorities and had Sompon released to him; whereupon, they informed Don that he was now Sompon Weah's father and his responsibility, if Sompon got into trouble, it is Don who would pay. It didn't matter. Don knew Sompon, saw him everyday, and saw him play his little humorous jokes that always left others laughing. It was Sompon who would drop by every night pulling out a magazine or a book pretending that he knew how to read, but didn't. Twelve years old is too young to pay such a heavy price; so Don adopted

Sompon and enrolled him in school. He also adopted Faka, whose father had died from malaria.

The country devil stood in the center of the fire peering into a glass of water he held in his hands. As he spoke, the flames began to gather their strength. He spoke of beating drums and powerful forces. He spoke of what he saw in the glass. He saw many cauldrons of boiling water and objects being thrown into them. He spoke of an uprising, and as the flames rode high into the night, his voice turned low and ominous, matching that of the heavy jungle beat. He spoke of Tuklo Whea and Bloba Doe being dragged from their huts. He spoke of fingers being chopped off, hands and arms being chopped off, he spoke of ears and lips being chopped off, and as he spoke, the fire grew brighter and hotter.

He spoke of heads being placed on poles and hearts being eaten raw. He spoke of countless merciless rapes, and as he spoke, he slowly raised his glass towards the sky before smashing it against the stones that encircled him, causing the flames to erupt into a moonless night.

"Don, wake up. Wake up Don." Someone was shaking him. "Wake up Don."

"What is it?" Don was sore and drenched in sweat from the jungle's heat and the malaria. He suddenly felt relieved, realizing that he had only been dreaming. Faka continued to shake him.

"Wake up, Don. Wake up."

"You can stop shaking me Faka, I'm up."

"You must get ready. Get dressed quickly; there is no time to wait."

"Slow down Faka. What the hell are you talking about?"

"Can't you hear the drums? They are coming. You must hurry."

Chea Dee removed her hand from Don's back and slowly rolled to the edge of the bed. Don ran his hand through his hair, turned, and looked at Chea Dee. She glanced at Don very quickly before rising to her feet. "Faka slow down. Who is coming?"

"The rebels, they have crossed the river and are headed this way. They are killing many people. The uprising has begun. They are coming. Listen. Listen to the drums."

Don heard the words and the drums, but they refused to make sense to him. He looked at Chea Dee who solemnly rubbed her swollen belly. She slowly began gathering a few of Don's things before quietly placing them into his daypack. "Go where?"

"Nyanti will guide you through the jungle and over to the sea. From there the fishermen will paddle you to safety. You must hurry. I'll wait for you outside."

Don turned to Chea Dee. She refused to look back at him. Don lifted himself from the bed and started to walk towards her. She turned away and stared out the window. Don silently stepped into his trousers and headed outside where Nyanti was waiting for him. "Nyanti, tell me what the hell is happening here."

"Faka told you everything. We really must hurry."

"What about you and Sompon? What about Chea Dee and…"

"Don't worry we will be safe."

"Safe! The way Faka tells it there is a major rebel force on their way here and they are going around chopping people up. What the hell do you mean it's safe? I need to take Chea Dee."

"She won't go."

"The hell she won't. I'll drag her if I have to."

"We have talked this over many times and this is the way it must be."

"We haven't talked. You've talked about it, not me. I am not leaving without her." Don looked around shouting, "Chea Dee. Chea Dee."

"She's gone. We must go now." Nyanti grabbed Don by his shoulder, staring him straight in the eyes. Don stood still as Faka handed him his bag.

Don stood exhausted at the water's edge, his arms and legs cut, scratched and bruised. It had taken them all night to reach this point. Don stood staring at the sea. He tried to stay but he knew that was not an option. The rebels were out for blood and his presence made the situation much worse. The drums had warned them of the impending danger, especially to foreigners, especially white foreigners. There was nothing he could have done. Nyanti was right. Nyanti said he and the others would be safe, the rebels were not after them; but he knew many years of violence were coming. Don tried to take Chea Dee and their unborn child but she wouldn't go. Nyanti said that taking her away from the village and the jungle would kill her. He was right about that too.

"Don."

"Yes Nyanti."

"You must go. Even here there is danger."

Don took one more look at the jungle, then stepped into the canoe.

MISTER ROOSTER

Rain pounded the tin roof of the mud hut with fist size droplets awakening Don from his chloroquine-induced nightmares. Chea Dee quietly slept by his side. What prompted Don to rise from his bed, just as the sun was letting the night know of its intent, was another reminder to him of how mysterious this place really was.

Don, trying to shake off the headache the anti-malaria medicine routinely produced, walked outside to the back of his hut where he encountered his current nemesis: the creature that had wreaked so much havoc in his life for the past three months, the creature that Don had fought countless battles with now stood helplessly in front of him, trapped at the bottom of the hundred-gallon plastic container Don had carried with him from the capital of Liberia. The rain continued to fall as the water slowly rose towards the creature's neck.

"Imagine me seeing you here," quizzed Don.

The creature, that was nothing more than an old nasty rooster, maintained his silent gaze on the water that fell from the roof and into the container.

"What am I going to do with you? Man have you caused me a world of troubles. I ought to go right back to sleep and just forget about you for the next hour or so, that'd solve a lot of my problems. Every single day you go running around humbugging my hens, you are really screwing up my project."

The rooster, seemingly indifferent of Don's presence, calmly looked down at the rising water that slowly inched higher.

"You look a little cold Mr. Rooster. I've tried everything possible to get you to leave my hens alone, but nope, you just have to have it your way. I guess it's not all your fault. That damn European rooster, although twice your size, he's just too young and stupid to have figured the whole thing out yet, but I still don't enjoy being brought up in front of the elders like that."

The early morning sun, fighting its way through the rain, gently painted the tree-topped horizon with bolden hues of yellow and gold. Don surveyed the rolling countryside and the scattering of mud huts his neighbors inhabited, only Weah's hut showed any signs of life as smoke slowly rose from his thatched roof.

"Listen Mr. Rooster, I really don't have anything against you. I know you're just doing what roosters do, but this project is bigger than you. That European rooster, who you so blatantly disregard as you go about your rooster business, is the one and only one who is supposed to be humbugging my hens. The idea is, and this isn't supposed to be a knock against you, is for his offspring to come into this world. They are going to be a lot bigger than yours. You should consider yourself lucky because if I had my way, I would have bought and eaten you a long time ago, but your owner, or master, or however you refer to him as, wouldn't sell you to me. Over time, I've tried giving you subtle hints, like yelling or throwing rocks and other things at you, but you're not the type to listen are you?"

The rooster cocked his head in an angle, casting a cold eye Don's way, and then simply opened and closed his mouth, before turning his attention back to the dripping water.

"Remember that little palava I had with all the neighbors and elders, the one where I had to buy all 'the something' for? You know, 'the something,' it's the local rum they brew in the jungle in old dug out canoes. Remember the meeting where I pointed out all the successful projects I've introduced to this place, like the palm tree orchard, the peanut farm and the swamp rice project. They all understood this as I explained it to them, and they thanked me for it too, but saying those words to Mr. Tweh sure put me in hot water. Pardon the pun if you will. Remember the time I chased you all the way back to your hut and, in my frustration, I yelled at

Mr. Tweh. That's right, that one. You know, I learned that phrase from him. I picked it up the time when, in a drunken rage over politics, he blurted it out to Charles Nyanti, but they didn't call a meeting then, did they. But they sure fired one up real quick when I told Mr. Tweh that he must have been the last monkey to fall out of the trees and put clothes on his back. I'm sure you were mighty pleased with yourself about it, too. That's the meeting in which you got Carte blanche to run around as you pleased and I was to never bother you again. Yeah, I know you remember that meeting."

The water tumbling off the roof had filled the container so that it now bridged the top of the rooster's chest. The rooster slowly moved his head up and down, watching and calculating his fate.

"I guess, however, I did learn something from it all. I learned Mr. Tweh was only keeping you because his aunt from a neighboring village was jealous of the whole project and wanted to undermine it."

Once again the rooster slowly opened and closed his mouth, a gesture that appeared to be, this time, more of a yawn than an insult.

"I'll tell you what Mr. Rooster, I'll make a deal with you. If I go fetch your owners so they can come get you out of this mess, you need to promise me one thing; you need to promise me that you will never humbug my hens again. You need to promise me that you are going to stay on your property and will never ever come over here again. Can you promise me that, because if not, I think I'll just go back to bed."

The rooster maintained his attention on the cascading waterfall. He seemed hesitant to answer. Don continued staring at him as the water slowly crept up his neck. The rooster quickly shifted his eyes towards Don's expressionless face before returning them to the container and the water that fell from the roof. Then the rooster blinked. Just once. That's when Don turned and walked to the rooster's house to fetch his owners. And, once again, calm and tranquility was restored to the quaint little African village.

HUNGER

This isn't why I was here. I joined the Peace Corps at the age of twenty-seven in order to help, but now I was the one in need of help. But maybe this is what the Peace Corps had in mind. Maybe in order to solve a problem, you first had to understand the problem. Well, I had a problem and I certainly understood what it was. I was hungry.

But I was more than just hungry. Back in the States all I had to do was go out and buy some food. Well, I had money, but there wasn't any food to be bought, not here at the end of the road. When I first arrived in Liberia, a small country on the west coast of

Africa, the Peace Corps handed me the name of the village where I was to be stationed, leaving the rest up to me. No bus ticket, no ride, no directions, nothing. Just "Here is the name of the village, and, good luck."

It took me five solid days of traveling over dusty clay roads before the truck drivers I'd hired finally dropped me off at the river's edge, where they politely informed me: "On the other side and just over that hill is where you will be living for the next two years."

A toothless old man, who I was to get to know very well, charged me a dime to carry me and my possessions across the river in a leaky dug out canoe that was as old, if not older, than he was. Two days later, the rains started.

In a week's time, the rivers had all filled and the clay roads that had previously been easily traveled over were instantly transformed into a giant winding quagmire of muck, swallowing and trapping anyone, or thing, brave enough to travel them. During the rainy season nothing moved, and it rained for six months straight. I was trapped in a village deep in the jungles of Africa. And I was hungry.

I've been hungry before, but I've never known hunger. A hunger brought about from going to bed hungry, waking up hungry and spending my days hungry. A hunger realized with having money in my pockets but nowhere to spend it. There was one small mud hut in the village where I could buy toilet paper, candles, canned sardines, tomato paste and a few other items; a store that quickly ran out of supplies as the rainy season unfolded itself. On Sundays, when it didn't rain, the village held an informal farmers market, supplying me with just enough food to reduce the sharp pain I felt in my gut to a dull, yet constant, agonizing throb.

As the rainy season progressed, my hunger gradually grew, transforming itself from an annoyance to something much more: It had taken root and began to bore itself into me. I was coming to the realization that hunger was, in actuality, a living entity. Hunger has a life of its own, similar to the worms, parasites and other organisms that invade and attach themselves to you; slowly and steadily feeding off of you until nothing is left but a shell of who you once were. I felt this hunger inching its way through me. I felt it as it migrated from my stomach and into my veins. I could feel this hunger slowly working its way through my entire central nervous system before finally planting itself dead-square-center in my brain, where it quickly began consuming and dominating all my thoughts.

Hunger, in a short amount of time, had become my closest and most constant companion. No matter where I went or what I did, hunger was always there, nagging me and reminding me of its presence: Like the girlfriend who you can't do enough for, the one who is terminally displeased and unsatisfied; such was my hunger, demanding more of me than I was capable of delivering. Hunger had developed a strangle hold on me.

Hunger refused to leave me alone, it even invaded my sleep where I suffered relentless dreams of the unquenchable feast, dreams of elaborate banquets where I dined and devoured the most wondrous of foods that the world had to offer; but a feast from which

I would awaken more famished than before with nothing in front of me but a small bowl of rice and okra soup. For countless nights I endured these dreams, dreams that would leave my gums bleeding and teeth marks in my pillow. Something had to be done about this hunger.

I decided to confront one of the local hunters, but when I first asked Mr. Weah to take me hunting, he refused, always talking about genies that lived in the bush. I told him that I didn't care, I'd eat anything, and I'd eat them too. But Mr. Weah was adamant, so I settled on buying him wire for making traps and snares. I also bought him shells for his old single shot shotgun. In return, I'd receive a portion of the spoils.

I soon learned that the hunting wasn't very good during the rainy season, and after waiting several weeks for Mr. Weah to catch something, I'd lost what little patience I still possessed. I informed Mr. Weah that if he wasn't going to take me hunting, I was going to stop supplying him with materials: I'd grown weary of holding a mosquito net over termite mounds, catching them as they flew out of their clay nests in a feeble attempt to add protein to my diet. Mr. Weah promised to take me hunting the first night it didn't rain.

"This is what you do," Weah instructed me. "You take this piece of inner tube and cut two vertical slits about this far apart. Now tie it around your head and slip the flashlight through the holes: This is your night-light. What I am about to tell you is very important, when we get into the bush, don't talk."

"I know, we don't want to scare off the game."

Weah gave me a stern look. "No. We don't want the genies to hear us. Make sure you stay within ten feet of me at all times. This is very important."

I am very skeptical of all this genie stuff, spirits living in the jungle and in the rivers and all that nonsense. Stories about how genies will trick you and lead you to your death and, possibly, turning you into a Zombie. If you do die in the bush, the villagers are forced to bury you out there. They say that genies are capable of entering and hiding in a dead person's body, allowing them to be transported across the protective JuJu barrier the witchdoctor has placed around the village.

Genies. Yeah right. Like I would believe in anything so silly as that. I was fed enough of those fairy tales in Catechism. Well, things can happen that will cause a person to change his or her mind, and what happened that night might simply have been the hunger manifesting itself into hallucinations, I don't really know, but I saw something, and it changed a lot of things. It occurred when Weah and I were about an hour into the jungle. He had spotted something on the other side of a small creek and signaled me to come closer. He slowly knelt down; concealing us from what ever it was that might have been out there. I felt the gnawing hunger in my stomach intensify.

"That meat?" I asked.

Weah put a finger to his lips. "Genie," he whispered.

I slowly raised my head and peered through the thick brush and could see a light about twenty yards away. "It's just another hunter." Weah placed his giant paw on my shoulder. I resisted his efforts and continued staring at the light. I watched the light traverse to my left then back towards the right. Then I saw the light shoot straight up in the air about ten or fifteen feet and then straight down. Weah jerked me to the ground burying my face in the mud. I felt a chill wind pass over me.

"What the hell is that?" I mumbled.

"Genie."

Hunched over, we slowly followed our tracks back to the main path from where we had come. Not a word was spoken as we walked under the thick dripping foliage. I stayed very close to Mr. Weah's heels as we put as much distance between us and whatever it was I'd just witnessed. It's easy to become lost in the jungle and not because there are a lot of paths winding their way through it, but because there aren't any posted signs of any kind telling you which path to take. Unless you know precisely how to reach your destination, it is very difficult to arrive safely, if at all, and I had no idea where we were.

The people here have a tremendous memory. They recognize every tree, every branch and every leaf. Where I was living, the oral tradition of story telling was alive and well. A storyteller would tell a story that could last an hour, and when he had finished, everyone listening could repeat the story verbatim. This ability they possess is extremely vital because they have no maps, nor do they write things down on paper. When given instructions on how to reach a particular place in the jungle, it is all given by oral instructions, and telling someone how to navigate through the jungle is very important. Remembering it is even more important.

Walking in the jungle's darkness that night, I could hear the drums talking between two distant villages. I have no idea what they are saying, but I felt within me some ominous beat. Weah and I continued on in silence, but as we hiked, I began to remember a trip I took with my friend Caba. He was summoned to an outlaying village to bring aide to a hunter who was injured by a dyker. A dyker is a small deer like animal with two spiraling horns protruding from its forehead. These animals are extremely dangerous when wounded. They will hide in the underbrush and wait for the hunter to approach. Then, they will ambush the hunter and drive their horns into them. This particular hunter had been lucky, having been merely gored in the leg.

It took Caba and me close to four hours before we reached the village where the injured hunter lay. Spanning the path of the entrance to the village stood a goalpost like apparatus. There was something wrapped in leaves and tied to the horizontal cross member.

"Caba, what is that?" I was pointing at the bundle.

"JuJu. The witchdoctor put it there to keep the evil spirits out."

"Does it work?"

"We're about to find out."

As we stepped through this spiritual barrier, the children playing nearby suddenly became aware of my presence and started running away, screaming and yelling, "Kupee, Kupee."

"What the hell is this Kupee thing?"

Caba was laughing, "You are."

"What"

"You are the Kupee."

"And that would be?"

"The Kupee is the walking dead. Parents tell their children that if they misbehave the Kupee will come and take them away. These kids have never seen a white person before. To them, you look like a ghost."

"I guess they must have done something wrong."

"Which child hasn't," Caba replied. "Or maybe they need a better witchdoctor."

"Very funny."

Country devils, witch doctors, genies and kupees. All kinds of strange spirits dwell here. I am finding out that I, too, am a very odd creature to the people living here. It's not entirely based on me being the lone white person living here but has more to do with their lack of body hair. I am basically a hairy man, especially when it comes to my belly hair, which curls up into tiny dread locks. Today, when people in the States comment on my belly, I tell them that before I went to Africa my body was completely bald; it was only after eating monkey while living in Africa that I started to grow so much hair.

My arms and legs are particularly hairy and the children, who weren't scared of the Kupee, would run up to me and start petting me the same way they would pet any other animal. They would run their hands about my arms and legs and say "O-you look just like monkey-O." My African girlfriends fondly referred to me as monkey-belly. At times, I felt like an animal in a petting zoo. Girls would come over simply to braid my hair. They would braid it, unbraid it and braid it again. I once had three girls braiding my hair and four or five kids petting me all at the same time. I was the village pet, the white monkey who lived under the almond tree.

Speaking of monkeys, I once walked into my neighbor's hut as he sat over a large cast iron pot filled with palm butter.

"What's that?" I asked

"That meat."

"I know that's meat. What kind of meat?"

"That monkey."

Did I eat monkey? Damn right I did. And I'll confess monkey is really good, scary good. I ate anything that walked, crawled, slithered, swam or flew. As I mentioned before, I even ate termites. I cooked them by tossing them into a pot of boiling oil. They had an interesting nutty flavor to them. To this day, I still refer to them as African popcorn. Like I said, if it moved, I ate it. If I saw a snake crawling across my path, I'd chase it down and fight it with my cutlass/machete, then I'd kill it and I'd eat it. And I ate them all; I ate them all because I was hungry. Crazy hungry: out of my mind hungry.

All of this was going through my head as Weah and I walked through the night. I was so lost in my thoughts that I almost ran into him when he'd abruptly came to a halt and whispered back to me, "When I give you the signal, turn on your lamp and point it down the path."

"Genie?"

"No, that meat."

For a brief and glorious moment I had escaped reality and my hunger. We had walked all the way back to the farm, an area covering acres upon acres that had been carved out of the thick African rain forest with nothing but axes and machetes. The first year they'd plant rice, followed by two more years in which cassava was planted. Not a single power tool amongst them. The men would cut and burn the bush, while the women did all the planting.

The Africa I know is a different Africa than most people are accustomed to seeing. Instead of the pictures depicting sadness and grief, images of downtrodden masses, the people here walked like Kings and Queens. They walked tall and proud, they moved eloquently and casually, they smiled almost constantly and were extremely generous, friendly and very social. They walked about with their heads held high, backs straight and erect, walking with a graceful effortless stride. They do this, in part, because they carry just about everything on top of their heads. They may use one of their hands to balance the load, but most of time, even that isn't necessary. A very common site is seeing a woman walking with a bucket of water on her head while holding hands with several children.

And this is the behavior I noticed most, the touching. Everyone always seemed to be touching someone. Touching is a constant here, not a variable. When in a conversation, they will hold hands, or, at the very least, constantly reach out and touch one another throughout the entire conversation. Touch is a fundamental and key aspect of the people's life here.

And when my African girl friends would touch me, calling me monkey belly…

I was thinking of this, too, when Weah had stopped, so I didn't hear the pigs rooting about the cassava plants until just now. However, my hunger promptly took notice and I was instantly on edge as I watched Weah slowly raise his gun and take aim, signaling me to turn on my light. And there they were, four big pigs, not more than sixty feet in front of us. I could sense my hunger's happiness as Weah fired the first shot, hitting the biggest pig in the front left shoulder. The distant drums that had lulled me to sleep earlier were suddenly drowned out by a horrible squealing noise.

Weah quickly cracked open the barrel of his single shot shotgun. I kept my light on the pig as it struggled to its feet. I now focused one eye on Weah, who is digging through his pocket, and one eye on the pig, which is fighting to regain his composure. I notice Weah pulling out a leaf and stuffing it into the barrel of the gun. The pig, on the other hand, has found his bearings and is staring straight into my light. I can see his wild violent glare as he starts charging forward. I can also hear my thoughts running through my brain: "Come on Weah, hurry up and shoot the damn thing." Mr. Weah methodically pulls a ball bearing out of his pocket, slipping it in behind the leaf. The leaf keeps the ball bearing from running out the other end of the barrel. The ball bearing is the slug.

The pig, despite his wound, has managed to cut the distance between us by more than half. I keep my light on him, capturing the anger in his grimacing face.

And as my flashlight illuminates the blood running off his shoulder and down his legs, I can feel the hair rising on the back of my neck. Weah dives back into his pocket fishing for the shotgun shell, and in my fear, I turn my attention to the trees. I am looking for the lowest and the closest branch I can climb.

I'm playing an eye game now, and there are three players involved: Weah, the pig and the tree. I am seriously thinking about the choices I have in front of me. I calculate my next move. I am going to run and climb the tree just to my left. I quickly glance at Weah who has just now located the shell. There's no time. I'm out of options. I'm going to run because that solid mass of angry-pissed-off-blood-spitting-beast is right on top of us. I can practically taste his rancid breath. I take a hard look at Weah as he shoves the shell into the barrel, snapping the gun closed. I'm not sure Weah can hit it, and if he does, I'm not sure he is going to kill it. I'm going to bolt. I'm headed straight for the tree before that horribly fanged animal rips us both apart.

But I can't run. I want to run, I know I should run, but I can't. And it's not because I am a brave man, or a loyal man or an honest man. None of these ideas or concepts keeps my feet solidly planted on the ground with my flashlight now firmly focused on the pig as it eliminates the last few feet between us. It is not cowardice, nor hate, nor meanness wishing for that bullet to hit its mark. It is one thing and one thing only keeping me here: Hunger, plain and simple.

I can still feel the adrenaline pumping through my body as I cut the pig up into smaller pieces. Weah, meanwhile, has calmly gathered some wood and has managed to start a fire. I load the body parts into two separate sacks. Weah walks over and cuts off several small chunks and places them into the fire. The smell of burning hair and flesh fills the air. Watching him cook the meat, I am taken back to the incident with the genie, because what I have just witnessed were the actions of a very brave and strong man who showed absolutely no signs of fear or panic, yet, in our encounter with the genie, I thought I saw a momentary flash of both. I begin to take JuJu a little more seriously.

The bargain Weah and I struck was that we would split the pig up between us. I naturally shared mine with Nyanti and his family. His wife Mary was honored to do the cooking. Well, when my fresh bowl of wild boar soup arrived, I could barely contain myself. Finally, I was saved. I took the first bite and quickly realized my mistake. Africans love pepper, hot melegueta pepper, and they use a lot of it. I quickly chewed and swallowed the first bite. Each sequential bite became an ensuing battle between my mouth and my stomach. Hunger would force the meat into my mouth against its will and objections. Hunger was commanding my mouth to chew and swallow despite my mouth's natural instinct and desire to spit it out. At some point, equilibrium was reached. I am still hungry.

Scars from the horror of my hunger still exist with me today. When I first returned from Africa I was almost arrested because I stood in the supermarket staring. I stood staring at the endless aisles of food where cereal alone has an entire section devoted to it. I stood mesmerized and transfixed for so long that the manager of the store thought I was completely stoned out of my mind and had called the police.

This hunger I experienced affects my life right up to the present moment. At restaurants, I will always take the leftovers home or, at the very least, hand it to someone outside who is in need of a meal. Friends or relatives who invite me to spend a weekend must inevitably contest with my habits, because, come Monday morning, the refrigerator will be loaded with leftovers. I just can't throw food away. Hunger won't allow it.

My friend married a Cuban girl who spent the first thirty years of her life on that Caribbean island. She tells stories of the great revolution that keeps practically everyone there on the brink of starvation while Castro hordes the rest for himself. To this day, ten years after the fact, this Cuban woman will keep her refrigerator stuffed full, overflowing full. Open the door and something will fall out. As soon as space opens up in the refrigerator, she'll fill it back up.

Towards the end of my two years in the jungle, another volunteer had decided he would visit every Peace Corps member at his or her site. Making it to my site was no small feat, so to honor such an occasion, I took him hunting with Mr. Weah. A couple of hours into the jungle we happen to stumble upon a marsh and as Mr. Weah raised his gun to shoot, our visitor yelled out, "Don't shoot, that's an endangered pygmy hippopotamus." Mr. Weah calmly called back, without ever taking his eye off the target, "That meat, that water pig, it's sweet, and me and my family are endangered." They say that a trapped or wounded animal is the most dangerous animal of all. I say the most dangerous

animal is a hungry man.

CABA

"They came in the night, I never heard them until the hens and rooster started making noises; by then it was too late." Don looked at the welts covering Caba's face and arms as he spoke. "My wife blames me." Caba picked a piece of Kola nut off the plate and rubbed it into the pepper and salt.

"Why's that?"

"She says I've become too westernized, says I've lost respect for the JuJu, I keep telling her that JuJu is nothing but a bunch of superstition." Caba and Don seemed to be going in opposite directions, for opposite reasons.

"So what happened?" Don watched Caba as he chewed on the Kola nut and reached for "the something." He knew Caba rarely drank, and when he did, it was usually only beer or palm wine.

"Hasn't Chea Dee shown you the right way to prepare the Kola nut?"

"I guess not."

"Where is she?"

"Went to the river to wash clothes."

"Very beautiful girl, but she doesn't know about the kola nut, what is needed is some paste added to the pepper, you shouldn't serve it like this. I can show you if you'd like?"

"Please do." Don followed Caba to the kitchen. "But tell me about last night."

Caba began digging around Don's kitchen, "I didn't pay much attention to the chickens; they will occasionally make noises in the night, but when the pigs started squealing, I knew something was up. By the time I got outside, all my chickens were done for. It was all I could do to save the pigs. My wife is very upset, keeps telling me that the attack was my fault. She doesn't understand that these things just happen. After all, they are only insects."

"But the welts, you're covered in them?" Don slowly incorporated the fact that Caba and his wife were from Lofa and that he had recently graduated from the University of Liberia in Monrovia as a physician assistant.

"The army ants had all but engulfed my chickens and had just started covering my pigs by the time I rushed into the pen and began knocking and mashing them off. You know these ants will first crawl on their victims and once they have gathered on him, they will go for the eyes and mouth, biting all at once, but they wait until the lead ants get to the eyes. I had a very hard time getting them off my pigs. Naturally they attacked me. I was able to herd my four pigs out of the pen, but I lost one pig as he ran into the bush."

Caba ran his fingers across the welts covering his forehead. "Here we are." He had found the Maggi cubes.

"They got all your chickens?"

"Ants got them all, by morning there was nothing left of them, not even the feathers." Caba unwrapped the cube, mashing it up with the pepper. "This is the way it is done." Caba took another kola nut and dipped it into the paste. "Here, try it now." Don took the kola nut and followed him back to the sitting room where Don's black and white cat laid; she was holding a small mouse in her jaws. Caba gently reached for the cat. She responded by taking a vicious swipe at him.

"That cat is a real hunter, be careful the fishermen don't take her; they'll sacrifice her to Dwin the water god for good luck."

"Not much I can do about that, but I'll try and keep an eye on her." Caba shook his head in approval as he reclaimed his seat. He removed some ointment from a small black bag he always carried with him and began rubbing it onto his legs. The knowledge of these bites began to be painfully aware to Don. Caba was a person who took a great deal of pride in his appearance, always wearing pants and button down shirts in public, but today he wore only shorts, a T-shirt and sandals.

"The Kru are like that though."

"What do you mean? Like what?"

"Like the palm wine. When the Kru extract the liquid from the palm tree to make palm wine, they always kill the tree, whereas the Kpelle, we know how to do it without killing the tree. It's the same with the pepper- few Kru use the Maggi cube."

Don noticed the displeased look on his face and wasn't sure if it was from the ant bites or from living here in Grand Kru County. He tried to answer his own question, "I think living in the eastern mountain region where the Krahn dominate would be worse. I traveled there just last month in an effort to help a horticulturist collect some rare plants. At one point, I ended up sleeping with a girl who had her clit cut out. What a horrific ritual that is."

"The Krahn are definitely the last monkeys to have fallen out of the trees and put clothes on their backs. This country and some of its practices, especially JuJu, can be absolutely brutal." Caba grimaced as he rubbed in the white paste.

Don decided he couldn't gauge the reasoning behind the swelling of Caba's face. Maybe it was both, the ants and the other things. "My fishery project in Grand Cess is a mess because of this JuJu business."

Caba simply raised and lowered his eyebrows in acknowledgment, dipping another Kola nut into the pepper paste.

Don continued his story, "They accused the mayor Samuel Toe of JuJu in the drowning deaths of two boys near Sass Town. They held him in jail until after the dry season so he couldn't brush his farm."

"Yes, I know that story. Even when the authorities investigated and said there was no foul play, his political rivals still insisted a witchdoctor be called in." Caba took another drink of "the something."

"What really bothered me about this," Don added, "was that I had gotten them a motor and a net for their canoe so they could catch more fish. All they had to do was go to Monrovia and bring the motor back. But instead, they used the money to pay for a witchdoctor."

"Mr. Toe was finally found innocent. Isn't that right?"

"Yes, but it was too late for him to plant rice."

Now Don had the pained look on his face. "Man is going to starve. Speaking of starving, I was able to buy a chicken yesterday, care to stay for lunch?"

Sompon and Faka had just returned from the river after helping Don's neighbor and landlord, Charles Nyanti, carry several bags of cement back to the hut. Nyanti was using the rent money Don paid him to modernize his house by pouring concrete slabs. By the time Don left this place, Nyanti was going to have a very nice house. The first time the two of them discussed rent, Nyanti made it very clear not to let anyone know the amount he paid. Nyanti was also extremely cautious in how he spent that money. He was leery of appearing as a Big Shot.

As Sompon and Faka, acting like brothers, went into the other room to retrieve the tied up hen, Caba continued the conversation.

"Did you know that President Samuel Kanyon Doe was the first tribal African in modern times to lead an African Country. All of our previous Presidents were all descends of black Americans who came over in the 1800's. That's why our capital is called Monrovia because your President at that time, James Monroe, funded their return."

"Yes, I learned that as part of our Peace Corps training." Don took a drink of "the something". He remembered the time when his bike was low on gas, and not being sure if he could make it to Harper, he threw a couple of bottles of the cane juice into his tank.

The bike never ran better. No wonder Caba rarely drank the stuff.

"Did they tell you that for most of our history only the Congos were allowed to vote? Up until Samuel Kanyon Doe, the Country were excluded from the democratic process."

"I'm confused."

"The Congos were originally the people who were in route to the Americas when slavery was finally abolished and the U.S. Navy, having intercepted some ships on the high seas destined for America, diverted them here. Before they arrived, the people from America were called Americo-Liberians. Everyone else was referred to as Country. After time, the Americo-Liberians allowed the Congos into the power structure, and ever since, they have both been referred to as Congo."

"That's ironic, free slaves landing here and denying the inhabitants the right to vote."

"Yes it is. Doe was considered a hero by ninety-five percent of the population when he first took power. The people celebrated wildly."

"What happened?"

"What almost always happens, he began to enjoy the power and began consolidating his and the Krahn's hold on Liberia, and then he began eating all the money, money given to him by the World Bank and other powers. Bribe money is what it is. Money loaned on the collateral of us. This is the World's story." Caba rubbed some more ointment onto his arms. "Before Doe overthrew Tolbert, who he brutally murdered, the

President of Liberia was a man by the name of Tubman, and what they probably didn't tell you at Peace Corps training was that after he died, they excavated under his mansion in Harper and found twenty-seven skulls buried beneath it, one skull for every year he was in office."

"JuJu?"

"Yes, JuJu." Caba swatted a 'No-see-em' with his African fly swatter, a fly swatter constructed of a bundle of needles approximately two-feet long with a final diameter of about an inch or two. Don's cat pounced on the wounded fly. Caba brushed the growling animal away. "Tubman's mansion is just past the Masonic temple as you head towards the harbor in Harper. Even today people are scared to walk near it at night. Things are turning bad again for many people here. This JuJu that people practice, especially the Gboyos, does a tremendous amount of harm."

"Gboyos?"

"Yes, this is the name for those who are involved in ritualistic killings. There is more of this going on than you realize. It's not just Samuel Kanyon Doe and his men who eat body parts for power."

"It was hard for me to believe what Samuel Kanyon Doe had done to Thomas Quiwonkpa after they captured him during his failed coup attempt. I heard they paraded him around town in the back of a jeep before butchering him, while he was still alive."

"They also sold his fingers on the street of Monrovia for people to make necklaces with. Half the city had necklaces, I've never heard of a man having a hundred or more fingers. As my country falls deeper into chaos, there will be more of it; JuJu, greed, hate and the lust for power is going to ravage my country for years to come." Don could see the worry in his eyes. "Unfortunately, this, too, is a part of our history."

Sompon and Faka finished plucking, cleaning and cooking the chicken, bringing it over to the table along with some rice, laughter and prideful smiles. They set the silvery colored pot in the middle of the table accompanied by four bowls and four spoons. Caba tasted the soup then stirred in the rest of the pepper paste from the kola nut plate.

"Who wants the feet?" The color in Caba's face began to return.

"Give them to Sompon; he did most of the cooking." Sompon gladly accepted them.

"And the head?"

"Give it to Faka." Now both were smiling and honored.

"My wife and I miss our hometown, but my country needs me here, and it is the only job available for me." Caba paused for a second to rub his wounds. "We are lucky to be this far from the capital. The Krahn are still taking their revenge for this coup attempt." Caba scanned the room in silence. Then he turned to Don with a forced smile, "Next week I must go on a vaccination program, would you like to come along?"

"How long will it take?"

"About two weeks. We'll hike to all the surrounding villages. It will be a very good trip for you."

"Sounds great."

"I would like to go, too. I would like to visit my village, it's been a long time since I'd last seen my mother." Faka was sitting on the edge of his seat.

"Yes, you can go, too, you can be of some use. We have a saying here, be very respectful of everyone you greet, you never know who they will be the next time you meet. I think this is why the people here have been quick to accept you, you seem to live by the same words." Don was proud of the compliment Caba gave him.

Sompon, who had polished off his soup, sat savoring the marrow of the bones he had just cracked with his teeth. When he had finished, he tied a string to a remaining piece of chicken bone and began leading the cat around the room. He started laughing aloud as the cat raced about trying to catch it. Caba thanked Don

for the meal and headed home, welts and all.

DIAMONDS AND GOLD

Don pushed his cat away from the snake it had

trapped in the corner of his kitchen. He could tell by the

brown and black diamond markings on its back that it

was a Cassava snake, more commonly known as a

Gabon viper. Many people here refer to it as the two-

step viper because after it bites you, you're dead within

two steps. And what a horrible death it is. Its venom

works by breaking down the blood vessels in the body,

causing them to leak and burst. Don had seen a few

victims of this snake's wrath, their bodies swollen and

bloated with blood leaking from their eyes, ears, fingertips and mouth. Don quickly grabbed a broom and his cutlass, and went about killing the three foot reptile.

"Looks like we'll being eating well today Orca." His black and white cat seemed upset at losing its playmate.

"Don't worry Orca, there's plenty more where they came from." Don lit the small kerosene stove that rested on an old wooden table and began boiling some water. He then turned his attention to skinning the snake. As Don peeled back the skin, Orca jumped onto the chair, twitching her tale in excitement and anticipation. She was constantly hungry now that she was feeding for more than one. As his cat patiently watched, Don chopped the snake into smaller pieces, tossing them into a pot of water. Since the rainy season had ended, the weekly farmers market had much more to offer, allowing Don to add some okra, a few other vegetables and pepper. He had grown accustomed to the pepper and sprinkled several teaspoons along with some Maggi cubes to his soon to be lunch.

"What's that?"

Chea Dee stood in the doorway of his hut holding a bucket in her hand.

"That meat."

"I know that meat, what kind of meat?"

"That snake."

"Oily meat, but sweet," Don scanned her face. She had the familiar markings of the Kru as two horizontal scars, each about an inch long, rested under her eyes. He slowly lowered his gaze, running it down her entire body, and then, just as slowly, he returned his attention to her solemn face, finally resting his eyes on her thick dark eyelashes. She wore the typical brightly colored African wrap known as a lapa. She also wore a white sleeveless cotton shirt, exposing her taunt slender arms. Chea Dee stared down at the cat.

"She has your eyes."

"What?"

"You and your cat, you have the same eyes"

"I guess so."

"When she gives birth, I would like one."

Chea Dee set down her bucket. Don watched as she brushed the cat off the chair and sat down.

"You like cats?"

"Cats catch mice, keeps them from eating the rice."

Chea Dee slowly scanned the sparsely furnished room that held nothing but a chair, a table and a few cooking utensils.

"You can have one. You want some soup?"

She calmly raised and lowered both eyebrows.

"Good, but it won't be ready for a while."
She caught him surveying her again. She slowly rose from the chair and picked up her bucket.

"I need to bring water to my house. I will come back."

"Good, I'll be here."

Don watched as she gently touched his forearm and moved towards the door.

"It's not good to have cat eyes"

"Why?"

"Cats are tricky and mischievous animals."

Chea Dee traced her fingers down his arm and then off his hand. Then she left to go bring water to her mother. Don's eyes followed her as she walked along the path leading to the river; he was admiring her graceful stride and the subtle swaying of her hips as she carried the bucket on her head, her arms dangling by her side. A stranger, who was approaching from the river, stopped her half way down the hill. Chea Dee stood talking to him for a brief moment before pointing up towards Don's mud hut.

Don watched the man as he struggled under the mid morning sun, his strides were short and choppy as he climbed the hill, his head hung over his torso, his eyes were focused on the ground immediately in front of him. It was a much different posture than that of the villagers who always walked with a slight arch in their backs, their heads held high and their eyes focused slightly upwards. The approaching man walked as though the burdens of the world weighed heavily upon him.

The breathless stranger extended his hand, his shirt and pants stained in sweat. "My name is Doctor Taggert Wilhiem, are you Mr. Don Hota?"

The man also lacked their effortless smile.

"Yes. Can I help you?"

"I sure hope so."

His accent was thick and hard, his clear blues eyes matching his blonde, yet receding, hairline. The redness on his face and arms indicated that this man was new to the jungle and its tropical sun. Don offered his visitor some water and booted the cat back out of the chair. Don waited for the stranger to gather his thoughts.

"I need someone to lead me to a special place in the bush."

"Why me? I am not an experienced guide. There are plenty of other men who will do that."

"This is partially true, but none of them can keep a secret."

"What makes you think I can or will?" The man looked somewhat dismayed. Don waited for his reply as he refilled his cup.

"The Lebanese told me." Don now knew what the man was going to say next and quickly cut him off.

"I know him, but I am not going back there. I am sure the Lebanese told you that, too."

The man pulled a photo from his wallet and laid it on the table. Don refused to look at it. "I need your help; she needs your help." Don leaned closer to the table and adjusted the flame on his stove.

"Did the Lebanese tell you what happened up there?"

"Yes."

"Now you know why I won't go back there."

"I'll pay you; pay you whatever you want."

"That's the last thing I want."

"Why, you have no desire for money?"

"Quite the opposite, but the JuJu up there is very strong and entering that area with those thoughts will definitely get you killed."

"Do you actually believe in this JuJu?"

"It's not a matter of believing or not. That's just the way it is. Even the witchdoctors won't enter that place, and for a damn good reason."

"What I am seeking is a cure for my daughter. I don't believe in JuJu but I believe that the plant you and the Lebanese brought back holds the key for saving my daughter's life. I have performed countless tests on the plant, but the active ingredient must have degenerated rather quickly because I came up with nothing."

"Maybe the magic of the plant has nothing to do with its active ingredient."

"Now you sound like the Lebanese. I need to go there and you're the only one I can turn to."

"That place is quite a distance from here and, besides, didn't he tell you about the leopards?"

"I'm not scared of cats."

"I'm not talking about cats." Don picked up the picture of the girl off the table. He didn't like what he saw. But what was he to do- travel back in there each and every time someone brought a picture of a sick child to him from the outside chance that this plant might actually hold some key ingredient to saving a life? Don handed the picture back to the stranger. He observed the man's trembling hands as he returned it to his wallet. Don was almost positive that this man could never make the journey. He also knew that if the plant had any chance of working, the man had to pick it himself. He was sure the Lebanese had told him that, too. Although Don was a caring man, he wasn't the sentimental type, and right now, he didn't like the feeling that was passing over him. Chea Dee was going to have to wait.

The two men made their way to the border town of Yekepa by way of money bus. It was while sitting in the back of a rusting pickup under a canvas tarp enclosure that Don learned that his traveling companion had been living in Liberia for the past three years doing research on the tropical jungle plants in the region. Don was surprised to hear that the Doctor had moved his family here from the safe haven of Europe. This forgotten country was no longer a safe place to be, especially after the rebels had captured the president, Samuel Kanyon Doe, who they brutally mutilated by first cutting off his ears, then an arm, then his legs, and then his penis and scrotum, before finally killing him and eating him. He wasn't surprised to hear, however, that the doctor spent most of his time in an air-conditioned lab. Don knew, though, that it wasn't brute strength that was required to make this journey. What was needed was a strong will, and Doctor Taggert Wilhiem, as Don was soon to find out, had a very strong will.

When Don had first made up his mind to help the Doctor, he dared not tell anyone in the village where he was headed, he merely informed them he was going into the mountains close to the Guinea border to visit some friends. This unsettled and troubled many of the villagers because of recent news of increasing violence in the region and, as he and the doctor passed through the village to begin their journey, he could hear them crying out loud in sorrow at his departure. It began to dawn on him that despite all the secrets that the jungle may have held, there seemed to be no secrets at all and, as he listened to them wail "Bwee-O" from their mud huts, a gesture that usually pleased him suddenly made him edgy and uncomfortable.

After leaving the money bus behind, the two men made their way to one of the many rivers that dissected the country. Don had decided that traveling up the river would be less conspicuous and much quicker than hiking the trails that wound their way through the thick African jungle. While paddling up the river, Don noticed that the Doctor, who sat in the front of the dug out canoe, was having a difficult time, so he offered up some friendly advice: "Tie off your pant legs and put on another shirt."

"Damn they hurt."

The doctor slapped himself for the umpteenth time.

"The 'no-see-ems' pack quite a bite, don't they? Tie off your cuffs, it will keep them from flying up your pant legs. Not only that, they can easily bite through that light shirt you're wearing."

The "no-see-ems" are a slender fly about an inch long. They are called that because they are always sneaking up on you, flying low to the ground and hiding behind whatever they can, even if it is just a shadow. Most of the time you never see them until it is too late. This is one of the drawbacks of traveling on the river.

"Keep your eye out for game, otherwise we won't be eating tonight."

Don kept his single-shot shotgun slung across his shoulder and back, content with dragging a hook and line behind him as they moved along the rivers edge. He had no intention of firing his gun, at least not for food. Both men had started out in silence, paddling with slow and deliberate strokes, which suited Don just fine. Occasionally, whenever he felt compelled to talk, the Doctor would break the peacefulness of the river by interjecting some scientific fact about their environment. Don sat patiently, waiting for the Doctor to run out of words, and although he tried responding with monosyllabic answers, or the simple gesture of confirmation by raising and lowering both eyebrows, the Doctor just knew too many words. It appeared that the further they traveled, the more enthusiastic the Doctor became. He seemed to be conducting his own little private tour. Don was hoping that the short statement about keeping his eyes open for game would keep the Doctor quiet. Unfortunately for Don, the botany lesson continued until they had reached their destination, on this second leg of their journey.

The two of them had made exceptional time, reaching the waterfall by three or four in the evening in what was normally a daylong trip. And although this was a good start, Don began to doubt the Doctor's words, and his story. Shoving these thoughts behind him, Don helped the Doctor drag the canoe onto the shore before they began cutting and gathering large leafs. They carried the leaves to a small cave hidden behind the falls and prepared to bed down for the night. In addition to the leaves, they also collected some firewood in which to cook the fish they had caught, and to keep the mosquitoes at bay. A local hunter had shown Don this particular spot the first time he'd made this dangerous trip. It was a safe place to camp for several reasons; the most important of these was that the leopard men didn't know about it. Showing it to the doctor was an example of just how secrets were lost, but he knew that tomorrow would be a long day and Don was in a hurry.

The next morning, after removing all signs of them having been there, they started following a path that went straight up the mountain. It was a path that was seldom used, not only because it was steep, but because it also led to a place very few people dared enter. The barely visible trail skirted the outer fringes of the devil bush, an area designated for secret society initiation rituals and, although many sections of the trail were completely obscured by heavy undergrowth, Don rarely used his cutlass to cut the brush, finding it to be too much like work. More importantly, however, he didn't want anyone knowing that he was here or where he was headed. The Doctor, who followed behind, was beginning to annoy him as he seemed to enjoy the exercise of cutting brush, but more than that, Don had picked up on his rhythm. The Doctor was marking the trail. Don could also hear the drums echoing below, his secret was out and so were the rebels. He turned to the doctor.

"We have to pick it up. We need to reach and cross the ridge by nightfall."

The doctor nodded his head in agreement. He appeared a tad winded but none so more than Don, who started feeling that uneasy chord resonating inside him again. He decided to test his apprehension and dramatically increased their pace. He kept the pressure on the entire hike up the mountain.

A thick fog clung to the ancient trees shrouding the ridge and the gorge below in a mist of wooden secrecy. Don filled both water bottles from the water that dripped off the wide leaves of the jungle foliage. His lungs and legs ached from the thinning air and the strenuous climb. He looked at the doctor gasping for breath as he sat on the ledge of a huge boulder. Don liked what he saw.

"Down there is where we need to go. We can ease up now; I doubt anyone is stupid enough to follow us in there. I doubt they will even come this far."

The Doctor forced a smile at the news.

The dense jungle became almost impassable as they descended down the steep walls of the chasm. Howler monkeys could be heard moving amongst the trees, their chatter increasing as the two men fell further into the green darkness. By nightfall, even the full moon had a difficult time peering into the abyss. At the bottom of this forbidden ravine, Don found a suitable place to make camp, and since the doctor liked to use his cutlass so much, he had him extend the perimeter of the small clearing. Don then pulled out a hammer and several spikes from his daypack and began driving them into four different trees. On each tree he placed two spikes as high as he could reach, spacing them about eighteen inches apart. He then stretched two horizontal strands between the trees, and in the middle of each pair of suspended rope, he weaved in the remaining pieces, forming two makeshift hammocks.

Don boosted the Doctor up into one of the hammocks. "Stay in your sleeping bag and keep yourself covered at all times. This is very important. No matter what happens, don't stick your head or any part of you body out. If you feel anything at all, a breeze or a weight on top of you, or if you believe you hear me calling you, don't move. Stay still and silent." The doctor shook his head as though he understood, but Don doubted that the Doctor took any of his warnings very seriously, especially those concerning the genies. Don then walked over to the other hammock and swung himself up. He took a tentative peek towards the dense fog as it crept down the massive trunks that supported the canopy above. Don hoped they weren't too late.

The jungle is normally very hot and humid but up here in the mountains, the nights can become extremely cold, and with the fog now engulfing them, it became almost freezing. As Don lay in his hammock, buried in his bag, he could hear the jungle and its inhabitants moving about. He never felt at ease when camping out in the jungle and he felt even more apprehensive being here. He'd seen and heard people mock JuJu and he'd also seen those same people experience horrific deaths. He tried blocking out the sounds of the jungle and his own troubling thoughts the best he could.

The last time he ventured this far in these mountains, he and the Lebanese, having already retrieved the plant they were after, were headed back to the river and, as they hiked through that area of the jungle known as the devil bush, they suddenly stumbled across a small group of men carrying metal claws and dressed up in leopard skins. Don and the Lebanese, seeking cover in the undergrowth, could see that they had captured a young man and two girls. The two of them, aware of the grave danger confronting them, cautiously crawled along the jungle floor until they

where no more than twenty feet away from the leopard

men and their prey. They watched as the leopard men

formed a circle around one of their victims, at which

point both men simultaneously raised their guns,

shooting two of the leopard men just as they swung

their metal-sharpened claws at the young man. The

three remaining leopard men were momentarily stunned

and surprised as they watched their accomplices get

blown apart by the shotgun blasts, but being jacked up

on JuJu and the Iboga root, they quickly turned and

attacked.

Don rolled along the ground and hid behind a

tree waiting for one of the leopard men who ran

screaming towards him. When the leopard man came

close, Don, making sure he stayed low to the ground,

sprung from behind the tree just as a metal claw slashed

through a moon-filled night, barely missing his head

and, as Don drove his cutlass deep into the belly of the

leopard man, the other claw came crashing down

ripping a huge gash out of the tree where Don had set

his trap. Don twirled around to see how the Lebanese

was handling his attackers and, if wasn't for one of the

girls chasing after one of the leopard men, the Lebanese

would have surely been gutted that night because

although he had managed to cut off the arm of one of

the leopard men, he couldn't handle both of them. As

the second leopard man swung his clawed arm in an

upper hook fashion, the girl unleashed her pent up fear

and fury with the help of a cutlass she picked up off the

ground and decapitated the leopard man.

Don still had no idea how they survived that dark night, but maybe, sometimes, fear and concern can be more of a motivating factor than anger and lust. The mere thought of that night still produced a great deal of anxiety in Don. Luckily, two of the leopard men's victims survived, but sadly to say, the other one died from his wounds before ever making it back to his village. His family had to bury him in the jungle. And with the outbreak of the civil war, the number of ritualistic killings had increased dramatically as many of the warriors were seeking extra powers. And as Don lay in his hammock, he didn't know if he was more frightened of the genies or of the leopard men. He finally decided that if he was going to die, he'd rather die in his sleep.

The eagerly awaited sun filtered its way down to the jungle floor painting it with scattering patches of oblong shapes and patterns where Don was awakened by the smell of smoke. The Doctor, having built a small fire, glanced over at him. Don stared at the doctor as he pulled a small metal cup out of the fire and stirred in some instant coffee. He didn't like the way the Doctor looked at him. Don eased himself out of the hammock and moved towards the fire where he sat directly opposite him. The fire gave off a welcoming warmth.

"Hope you don't mind, I was cold."

"How did you sleep Doc?"

"Very soundly"

"Good. We should be able to find what you're looking for today and hopefully be out of here by tomorrow." Don measured the Doctor's reaction through the smoke.

"I will be very happy about that." The doctor poked the fire with a stick. "Shouldn't we get going?"

"Good idea." Don set about breaking camp and as he packed the ropes into his day pack, he checked to make sure his shotgun was loaded and ready.

The two men followed a narrow trail carved out of the bush by the animals, leading them both to the creek below. During the rainy season the creek was a raging river that slowly ate away at the mountain, thus exposing its secrets. Now, however, it moved at a gentler pace and, as they climbed over the rocks, Don heard the Doctor calling out for him to stop. The Doctor was holding a pistol.

"What's that for?" The Doctor was giddy with desire as he stared down into a small pool of water. Below him diamonds flickered in the sun. He reached down into the water and shoved a few into his pocket. "I wouldn't do that if I were you."

"What, going scare me with that JuJu bullshit. Now place the gun and the cutlass against the rocks." Don slowly did as he was told. The Doctor reached into the water again. "Beautiful, absolutely beautiful."

"You're going to shoot me?"

"Only if I have to. Now, step into the stream. That's it, keep going until you're up to your waist."

"You won't make it out without me." The howler monkeys that had been following them from the safety of the trees appeared agitated and started making noises.

"Don't worry, I can find my way out if necessary." The Doctor tucked the gun into his belt and pulled a bag out of his daypack.

"So what's your real story, obviously you aren't a doctor."

"In a way, I am, but to answer your question, I used to do business with the Lebanese. Well, one night after drinking too much, he let it slip out about this place, and with a few more poignant questions, he pretty much told me all I wanted to know, except how to get here."

"So why me?"

"Believe it or not you're one of the few men who knows how to get here, and is willing to go. And like the Lebanese said, you know how to keep a secret."

"And the little girl?"

"Just a photo I took. The Lebanese also told me about your one weakness, you care too much."

"And the Lebanese?"

"He doesn't have any more worries." The Doctor continued to fill his bag with the precious stones.

"I'm telling you, leave them there."

"I'll give you a cut, a very small cut."

"I don't want anything to do with it."

"What, more JuJu stories and fairy tales." The Doctor worked his way around a boulder, spying another handful of diamonds that lay under a small log. The monkeys began to scream louder.

"Think whatever you want," warned Don.

"What's up with the monkeys?" The Doctor pulled out his gun and shot into the trees, "Take that you noisy bastards." He fired off another round. "And here's one for your damn JuJu."

The Doctor didn't see it as he scrambled for the riches that lay at his feet; he didn't see its brown and black-checkered back blending in perfectly with the log. Then the snake struck. The Doctor dropped his gun, jerking his punctured arm away from the fangs of the two-step viper. Then it struck him again. The Doctor looked at Don with a surprised expression glued to his face as he tried to move forward, his legs trembling and twitching from the poison and the fear of knowing what was going to happen next. Don could see the Doctor's eyes beginning to fill with blood. He calmly watched as the Doctor fell over backwards, his limp body convulsing on the rocks as the river slowly slipped over him, his eyes staring blindly up at the sun, his mouth opening and closing in a whispering gurgle, diamonds spilling out of his hands and finger tips, dripping with blood.

Don walked into the morning glow of the village where several children came running to welcome him home. They held his hands, petting his hairy arms until they reached the boundary of their parent's gaze, before passing him off to another group of kids. His neighbors stood in the doorway of their huts waving and smiling at him and, as he walked up the path to his hut, he met Chea Dee carrying a bucket of water on her head. She reached out and gently stroked his forearm, resting her fingers in his hand. Once again, she caught him surveying her. A warm effortless smile spread across her face as she calmly raised and lowered both

eyebrows.

SNAKE Proof

How many people do you know who are snake
proof? Well, you can add one more to your list, because
I am. And how did this all come about? It all started
when Caba and I went on a two weeklong vaccination
expedition covering all the local surrounding villages.
This is a yearly program sponsored by the Liberian
government and the United Nations Development
Project. Since there are no roads where we are
venturing to, we travel by foot deep into the jungle and
deep into JuJu.

A week into our trip, we entered yet another remote village, but at this particular village we first had to make a visit to the witchdoctor. There is nothing, nor one thing, that singles out who he is except the reverence given to him by the others and a bracelet he wears: a bracelet that bears no clasp or any other visible signs indicating how it came to be attached to his ankle. He encourages me to examine it. I find nothing. The rumor is the genies put it there, thus attesting to his powers.

Upon entering his hut, we are invited to sit down but there are no chairs. In the far corner of the room, I notice a peculiar flat round rock, so I walk over to it, and, right as I am about to sit down, the witchdoctor grabs my arm enlightening me that if I were to sit there, it would create a big problem for me. The rock is, in essence, his throne. He tells me that no one has ever sat on that rock, except himself. I am told it holds very powerful JuJu.

By this juncture of my Peace Corps experience, I am fairly well versed in the JuJu belief, but I'm still finding out new fascinating and interesting aspects of this thing they call JuJu. I talk at length with the witchdoctor about this JuJu and he politely answers many of my questions. One enlightening story he tells, which quickly peaks my interest, is that of a senator who was running for re-election in Maryland County. The senator was charged with the disappearance of several young boys who the crowd suspected where victims of JuJu. The senator, of course, vehemently denied these accusations of being involved in the boys' disappearance and of the charges of performing JuJu. That was until he, the witchdoctor, proved otherwise.

He had been called in because this particular case involved very powerful JuJu and only a few witchdoctors were strong enough to see into the magic. He assembled the people, along with the senator, and performed his ritual; whereupon, he peered into a glass of water he held between his hands and began describing to the crowd what he saw in the glass and what the senator had done.

The senator, realizing the witchdoctor's power, dropped his pretense of innocence and confessed to his crimes. He confessed to cutting off the lips of his victims, to cutting out the skin beneath their armpits and tossing their parts into a cauldron of boiling water. He also confessed to gouging out their eyes, ripping out their throats and dismembering them while they were alive, and, finally, to eating their hearts, livers and intestines. The senator, having given his gruesome account of the event, begged for mercy. There was to be none that day and they hung the senator and his accomplices by the neck until they were dead. Then they kept their bodies strung up in the middle of town for several weeks, thus sending a strong message to anyone else who may have been thinking about performing such JuJu in attempts to gain more power.

The witchdoctor told many other disturbing tales that day. I soon learned that Liberia was full of secret societies such as the Leopard Society, the Crocodile Society and the Devil Society, just to name a few. I also learned that their members filled the ranks of government. To me, they appeared to be a raw version of the Skull and Bones Society. This is when the witchdoctor turned to me and asked if I wanted to become snake proof.

I was initially caught off guard by his question, especially after the tales he had just spun, but when he asked me for the second time, I thought to myself, now how cool would that be? So I asked him, "What does it take to become snake proof, would I have to chop or eat anyone?"

He assured me it didn't involve anything of the sort: I was not to be a Gboyo. Essentially, it came down to paying him a hundred dollars. I am thinking this is a fairly stiff price, but since there isn't anything else for me to spend my money on while living in the jungle, I should jump at this unique and intriguing offer. The witchdoctor tells me it will take some preparation and, since Caba and I still needed to complete our mission, we settle on a date two weeks from the day.

The omens I received on my hike back to the witchdoctor's village were very positive. While walking on the path that cut its way through the jungle, a giant tree fell not more than twenty feet behind us. Faka, who was leading me back into the bush, exclaimed, "We are walking at just the right pace, any slower and we would have been crushed." On the same path, not more than thirty minutes later, a deadly green mamba raced across our path and, once again, Faka pointed out the now obvious fact, "We are walking at just the right pace, any faster and we would have run into that snake." As Faka and I continued on this rather long day of hiking, drawing us ever so nearer to the witchdoctor, we happened upon a hunter beaming with pride. And, as is the custom when hiking through the bush, we stopped and said our hellos before striking up a conversation with him. He started telling us of his futile attempt at hunting that day when he suddenly came across a giant boa that had recently finished consuming a small calf. He told us, if we helped him carry his good fortune back to the village, he'd be extremely grateful and would put us up for the night. Faka and I looked at each other; we were walking at just the right pace. Yes, the omens were good.

The snake proof ceremony began with us and an entourage of others being led by the witchdoctor, at evening's twilight, to a clearing carved out of the jungle about an hours walk from his hut. I wondered aloud why we had to travel so deep into the bush and was informed by Faka that the JuJu necessary for becoming snake proof is very powerful and cannot be performed too close to the village. At one end of this clearing someone has piled a rather large amount of wood. The witchdoctor, walking to its edge, waves his arm over the pile of wood, igniting it instantly. The large bag of Kola nuts we carried with us were laid out and cut into smaller pieces. These pieces were then placed on a large plate with an ample amount of salt and a very strange looking pepper based concoction. It tastes very different from what I am accustomed to. Faka also notices this; it is the taste of the Iboga root. Next to this plate, they set down several large plastic containers holding water, and "the something". The drummers, forming a semi-circle on the outer edge of the clearing, began drumming.

The Kola nut is extremely bitter when chewed and I assume this is the reason for the salt and the pepper paste. The first thing you do is dip the nut into the salt, then into the paste, followed by a glass of water and a shot of "the something." This ritual, along with the drumming and dancing, continues on for hours, never pausing, not even for a second: More Kola nut, more something, more drumming and more dancing. Before long, I begin to feel myself falling into a light trance. I begin wondering, "how long have I been at it," and I fully realize that time is a relative matter, especially here in the jungle, but I'm beginning to feel as though time itself has stopped.

The longer I stay and live here in the jungle, the more time itself keeps changing its meaning and importance. I am beginning to think that I've been here too long because I have no idea what day of the week it is, neither am I sure of the month. Time is passing almost unabated- the days of the week simply marked by the weekly farmers market; the months denoted and determined by the rainy and dry seasons. The calendar has lost its importance. Chunks of time are no longer broken down into finite little packages, no longer reduced to fifteen-minute intervals. Time is no longer carved up and dispersed in desperate intervals dictated by winding hands pounding out digital seconds driving our modern day lives. I'm beginning to enjoy this newly found freedom; a freedom spawned where wearing a watch has become meaningless. There are no schedules to maintain or dead lines to meet- just a slow passage through lingering days and silent nights, both which are occasionally interrupted by the talking drums; day's beginning with a rooster's call acting as life's alarm clock; a day's pace set by footsteps, not by trains or cars. Time has developed new parameters, new patterns and new pressures: Such as brushing the farm, and planting rice and cassava. And as this particular night grows older, what few benchmarks may have existed, have completely disappeared, even those imposed by my hunger. All of them have been stretched thin to the point of disappearing, except for one: they keep me dancing to the drums.

The fire is kept alive by continually adding fuel to it, and the shadows being projected onto the dense foliage are contributing their own surreal dimension to the entire scenario; shadows appearing, at times, more real than the dancers themselves. I begin to acquire a very strange sense of abandonment as I spot my shadow dancing in the dirt, a solitary figure steadily making its way to the green curtain hemming us in; and although I believe I should be tired, having danced non-stop in a single place devoid of time, neither I, nor my shadow, are tired. I am being pulled deeper into the night and into JuJu, dancing to the drums.

At what appears to be some arbitrary point in the ceremony, the witchdoctor has suddenly decided that his little parlor game has gone on long enough, and with a peculiar sense of detachment, I watch him as he lifts himself up from the ground and walks towards the fire's edge. I notice him moving, yet he has taken on a very odd appearance, and it's difficult to accurately describe how he looks, but it is similar to a movie when the film, having been dislodged from the projector's spokes, flickers across the screen in broken fragments, where, at alternating intervals, the witchdoctor is more animal than man. This sensation comes in waves, first in tiny ripples that spread through my entire body like tiny tremors, slowly evolving into a streamless sense of consciousness, finally ending in one giant cascading fall, leaving me and my shadow attached again, and the witchdoctor in his human form.

With his back to us, the witchdoctor begins to speak to the fire and the jungle, but I can't understand the words, they are being mutated by the beating drums. I ask Faka to translate their meaning to me. Faka's garbled words confuse me further, words of gibberish that are occasionally interrupted with the only word distinguishable to me: JuJu. Faka's smile melts to a distorted grin engulfing his entire face. I feel the ripples beginning to rush through me again. The witchdoctor spins around to face me, whipping his reptilian tail through the flames and behind him, sending sparks into the dark abyss above us.

Silence. Complete silence. Nothing. The drums have stopped beating and the witchdoctor has stopped talking. Even the jungle refuses to make a sound. Sharpened scaly nails gently push me towards the center of the ring, towards the witchdoctor. The witchdoctor passes his arms over me while reciting a few incantations. Then he turns and walks away, his crocodilian tail disappearing into the dirt and dust. The waves that had engulfed me begin to subside. I can also see Faka's smile slowly returning to its natural proportions. I now assume I am snake proof. I, too, start to walk forward. Faka stops me: "Wait", he says. Then they come.

Earlier, several men had left the ceremony, however, being caught up in the ceremony, I never noticed them leave, but I see them now as they are re-entering the clearing. Bodies painted in white mud, and carrying straw baskets on top of their heads, move to a forbidden rhythm, tossing their contents onto the ground in front of, and around me. I feel the flames from the fire branding my back, flames whose heat stretches out towards my rebellious shadow; a shadow caught clinging to the jungle's edge, a shadow no longer attached to my ankle.

I am told to walk. I am told to walk through a sea of snakes that lay squirming and hissing in the dirt. My shadow beckons me forward, so I walk. I walk because I am high. I am high on the drums, the rum, the dance, the root and the nut. Mesmerized and held by this strange and magical trance, I begin inching my way through them, knowing exactly where and where not to step. I pause. I look at the slithering creatures moving about my feet and I can hear them talking with flickering tongues and guttural hisses. I feel a rhythm inside me, but the drums remain silent. I place one foot in an area vacated by a brown and black "diamonded" snake, while another larger snake, shiny and black, slithers around and over my boot, his rapid tongue tasting their leathery shoelaces. I sense an alarming-aggravating vibration approaching from behind, forcing me to pivot and turn. The leaping fire illuminates the path in front of me. A bright green snake with an orange throat is racing across the other reptiles and towards me, and as it closes in on me, it strikes, barely missing my elbow. I hold my ground as the other serpents react to his rage, a chorus of opening mouths and exposing fangs hiss and strike at the night air, the deadly green mamba quickly and shamefully retreats, escaping into the night, escaping into the jungle. I start walking again and, as I wade through this pool of serpent flesh, a strange beat resonates within me. I am walking towards a distant shore that lies on the other side of these limbless creatures. I am walking towards my shadow. I am now snake proof.

The next morning, now that time has found itself again and its mechanisms fully restored, now that my shadow has regained its lawful and dutiful place by my side, I can't help but feel that the night before was nothing more than a weird-wild exotic dream, that's when I see the witch doctor approaching, and he asks me: "Do you want to be bullet proof?"

WAH-WAH WOOD

"No-one can surf here."

"Why do you say that?"

"Just look at it."

"Where are you from?"

"Pennsylvania. Why do you ask?"

"Just curious."

This is what I mean: I'm from California and I'm sitting on a beach in the jungles of West Africa looking at waves no bigger than head high and some cat from Pennsylvania has an opinion on what can and can not be surfed.

"It's a mute point anyways."

"Why's that?"

"No one here has a surf board."

I repeat: I'm sitting on a beach in the jungles of West Africa with some cat from Pennsylvania who has no idea that at this very moment I have a board that is just about finished. I am only waiting for the marine varnish to dry. And this is what I am talking about and you should know exactly what I mean. If not, well, then I'll tell you. I remember as a child my father saying to me, "What's the use of cheating or copying someone else's work, all you are going to do is learn their mistakes. What you need to do in this life is make your own mistakes and learn from them. But, most importantly, never let anyone tell you what you can and cannot do. Find out for yourself."

How did I get in this conversation with a Peace Corps volunteer from Pennsylvania? More importantly though, how did I go about getting a board made here in the jungles of West Africa? I guess it all starts with the man who helped me make my board, and that would be Abraham.

I met Abraham, woodworker/craftsman, through another Peace Corps volunteer by the name of Dean. I was helping Dean at the Leper colony along with a Catholic priest by the name of Father Jay. When I told Dean of my plans to build a surfboard, he immediately told me about Abraham.

"So you can make me what I want?" I ask this question as I'm spreading out a photo of some old classic long boards from a surf magazine I had brought with me. I assumed that the Peace Corps wasn't going to be too receptive of me bringing my surfboard to Africa, so I brought along a magazine. That way, I figured, one way or another, I could get one made.

"Before I started making these other things," Abraham waves an arm while leaning over a wooden table that stands in the middle of his cluttered mud hut/work shop, "I used to build boats in Nigeria. The most important thing here is to get the right wood. Not any wood will do." He's speaking around a cigarette hanging from his lips.

"Oh yeah. And what wood do we need to make this surf board?"

"We need the Wah-Wah Wood."

"You're kidding me, the Wah-Wah Wood."

"Yes, the Wah-Wah Wood: it's very light and strong."

"O.K., how do we get this Wah-Wah Wood?"

"I know of some people. I will let you know when we can travel and get this wood."

"Perfect," But how is he going to let me know when it's time to go get this Wah-Wah wood? I have no clue. I try asking him but he just gives me a puzzled look as if I'm crazy. I leave it at that and return back to my site, which is a half-day's ride by motorbike. Luckily for me, the United Nations supplied me with a bike so I could perform my duties. Unfortunately, due to the rains, I wasn't able to operate it for six months. But that's another story for another time. The point being is I'm going to get a board.

About a week goes by before Charles Nyanti knocks on my door and tells me that I'm to go to Pleebo. I ask Nyanti why and he merely says that the drums have sent a message telling the Kupee that he is to go to Pleebo. And then it dawns on me; Abraham has found the Wah-Wah Wood.

For those of you who are a tad confused, let me explain. Where I was living, the talking drums still existed. I spent many nights in my mud hut listening to them echoing through the jungle as people from distant villages talked to one another, talking via these giant drums, drums large enough to sit on, drums beating out a message in a language far more complicated than anything Morse ever came up with. Not a bunch of dashes and dots tapped out on fingertips, but a permeating rhythm pounded out and absorbed by the jungle. Drum sounds that told the clearest of messages, messages I would never be privy to, except for those drums telling me that Abraham had found the Wah-Wah Wood.

And who or what is this Kupee? Well, Kupee roughly means the White man. The literal translation means ghost or the walking dead; since I am the only Kupee within a thirty-mile radius, it was easy to figure out whom the message was intended for.

Pulling up to Abraham's workshop, he calmly informs me, cigarette still hanging from his lips, that some of his friends are harvesting some Wah-Wah Wood and that we're in luck in that it isn't too far from where we're at, probably three days at the most. So off we go, in search of the Wah-Wah Wood.

Traveling across Liberia is usually accomplished by either walking or taking a vehicle called a "money bus", which is basically an old Toyota pick-up held together by bailing wire and duct tape. There are four vertical steel posts welded to the four corners of the bed with several horizontal bars attached to them forming a cage. Draped over this cage is a canvas top and inside this makeshift tent are two unsecured wooden benches. The thing is, "the money bus" won't leave until the driver has a certain number of people. I have spent days waiting for a "money bus" to leave a station, which isn't a station at all. The driver merely parks in a central location and waits until enough passengers are willing to go. Luckily for us we were able to leave by midday.

The "carboys" grab our gear as they encourage everyone to keep "dressing down," meaning to keep scooting along the bench so more people can get in. Today, I think they are trying to set a Guinness World Record. The road we are on is humorously referred to as the Liberian highway, a clay road carved out of the jungle by logging companies so they can carry their loads to the three shipping ports located on the coast. The road is littered with potholes and ruts, and during the rainy season this brick-hard road is transformed into an impassable muddy quagmire. Riding in the back of these torture chambers is akin to being stuck below in a crowded boat as it bounces over the ocean. Whenever I travel by "money bus", at least one person will inevitably become car sick and such is the case today as an old woman frantically keeps swiveling her head back and forth, until, finally, resting her gaze on me with that all too familiar expression. I quickly untie the canvas flap and direct her head outside. Today I am fortunate as her breakfast of boiled cassava and smoked fish dribbles off the side of the dusty pickup.

The "money bus" drops us off just a few hours up the road where Abraham and I follow a trail leading away from the road and into the bush. We hike until dark, finding refuge in a village nestled against a stream. The luxury of staying next to a stream is a welcomed gift because Liberia can be extremely dusty and hot. And this is something else that amazes me, while I seem to be constantly covered in a film of red dust, or red mud when it's rainy season, the people here always appear clean. They could wear white pants in the middle of rainy season and never have a speck of mud on them. Maybe I need the JuJu that will make me mud proof.

Swimming in the stream after walking all day provides a pleasant relief from the stifling humidity of the tropical jungle. Abraham isn't too keen on the idea and stays close to shore as I swim out towards it center where the current is swift enough allowing me to swim in one spot. The other great advantage to being next to a stream is they usually have fish or some other variety of game. The last the time I went trekking through the jungle I was headed towards a village where I was working on a peanut project. They honored me that night by serving me smoked bat and rice, the bat welcoming me with open wings and open mouth. Well tonight was to be different as we dine on something much more pleasant. A local hunter has killed some fresh meat and we are treated this evening to some crocodile soup. I give a quick glance towards Abraham and I begin wondering where exactly did this hunter capture it. The hunter calmly points in the direction where we had been swimming. The people around me start laughing. I don't think it's funny. I learn that anyone catching a crocodile must inform the witchdoctor, and the penalty for not informing him is steep and bitter. The bile, once removed, is entrusted to him. It is an extremely poisonous substance and is often used in their JuJu practices.

Tonight they have cooked the meat in palm butter. It is obtained by boiling and beating an African palm nut with a mortar and pestle. After squeezing the fiber and nut, there remains a thick orange substance that is allowed to sit, thus separating out the lighter transparent red frying oil from the heavier palm butter.

Add some pepper, the meat you want and you have yourself an excellent meal.

In Africa I was perpetually hungry, having, at one point, been reduced to holding a net over termite mounds in order to catch them as they flew out. I would toss them into a pot of boiling palm oil producing a nutty flavored meal jokingly referred to as African popcorn. I quickly took up hunting and if it moved, I ate it. Many times I have crossed paths with a snake, usually in my house or in the outhouse where I had built a water seal toilet. I killed these venomous vipers with a cutlass and then, I ate them. After my first encounter with a snake, I made it a habit to always carry a cutlass. I did this out of safety and hunger.

I built a water seal toilet because where I was living they had nothing but a small cross bar held up by two vertical sticks which I had to sling my ass over to take a dump, then watch as a million flies descended upon it. There was no way I was going to live like that, let alone having flies crawl all over my food afterwards, which is great way to get amoebas. And I've witnessed people suffering simultaneously from both malaria and amebas, watching helplessly as malaria weakens and cripples them with its fever and bone crushing pain, watching them struggle as Montezuma's revenge delivers its knock out punch. It's an ugly site. In my travels, I've come to the belief that the fly and the mosquito are the devil's pets, and although they may be important creatures in the scheme of things, they're the devil's pets, nonetheless.

The next morning, Abraham and I decide to get off to an early start. If we push all day, we should be able to reach the place where the Wah-Wah Wood is by nightfall. Before I joined the Peace Corps, I was living in Santa Barbara and working at a local restaurant. Restaurant work is good work for a beach/surf bum as it puts cash in your pocket and frees up your days to enjoy the more pleasurable aspects of life. I was riding my bicycle thirty or more miles a day, swimming or surfing every afternoon, and playing volleyball in the evenings, but I can't keep up with Abraham as we hike through the jungle. He is thirty years older than me, has the perpetual cigarette hanging from his lips, yet it is I who must call out several times for a break.

We reach our destination sometime after dark. Being thoroughly exhausted, I begin unrolling my sleeping gear under the nearest tree I can find when

Abraham suddenly stops me, "We must ask the trees for their permission."

"What's that, we have to ask the trees for their permission?"

"Yes, we are in a very magical place right now, there's heavy JuJu here, and being in Zoe country, it's essential we ask the trees." I watch Abraham as he very methodically goes around and starts talking to the trees. He is speaking a dialect I am unfamiliar with so I have no idea what he is saying, but I am beginning to wonder what it is he is really smoking. After talking to several trees, Abraham finally finds a suitable place for us to bed down. He tells me, "In this part of the jungle, if you were to sleep under the trees without their permission, they would kill you in the night as you slept. They could strangle you with their roots or just crush you with their limbs, but if you ask them, then they will protect you."

"Are you sure it's O.K. to sleep here?"

"Yes, I am sure, and they've promise to protect us from the crocodile men."

"The what?"

"The crocodile men. That's the name of the secret society that inhabits this area. You don't know this?"

"I don't know anything about talking trees or crocodile men."

"They perform the worst JuJu; they are Gboyos, people who do the ritualistic killings"

"You're telling me a bunch of men are running around dressed like crocodiles kidnapping and killing people."

"And eating them?"

"And eating them! What the hell are we doing out here then?"

"We are here to get the Wah-Wah Wood. Don't worry, the trees will protect us."

"Good, I feel a hell of a lot better now." This is early on in my Peace Corps experience and I am not too familiar with JuJu or its importance, but the first time I had cut my hair and clipped my finger nails, my neighbors made it very clear to me that I needed to burn them because if someone was to get hold of these items, they could cast JuJu on me. Right now, I'm not feeling all that comfortable with this JuJu business.

The next morning, after a very long and sleepless night, I was grateful to be alive and thanked the trees for their generosity and hospitality. From there,

Abraham and I hiked the remaining distance to the place where his friends were cutting timber. It didn't take Abraham very long to find a suitable log and we quickly began sawing out a plank for my Wah-Wah board. The saw was a giant two handled ripping saw and by noon we had successfully obtained, what Abraham called, the perfect Wah-Wah plank. Enlisting the efforts of two of the workers, we carried the plank out of the bush.

At Abraham's mud hut/workshop, we set about making my board. First, we outline the general shape with charcoal. Then, we hand saw the plank while using an axe to get the right camber. After that, we plane the board smooth. Abraham then re-uses the ax on the top portion of the board making a rough surface along its entire length to help prevent me from slipping off.

Abraham has fashioned a fin from some mahogany and attaches it by chiseling out a channel and gluing it in. I now have my eight-six round nose Wah-Wah board. All we have to do now is apply several coats of marine varnish and I'm ready for surf.

I'm not trying to brag here, well, ok, maybe a little, but I believe I am the first person, and maybe the only person, to have ever surfed this particular area of the world. In Monrovia, before the civil war broke out, there were a few Embassy kids who surfed, but I doubt they ever made it this far south. While in Monrovia, I occasionally went surfing with them and I asked them a lot of questions about the surf in the surrounding area, but none of them ever confessed to having come even remotely close to where I was living, nor did they know of anyone who had. In all my years, outside the handful of surfers living in the capital, I have never heard of anyone surfing in Liberia

The villagers where I am surfing are also telling me they have never witnessed anyone else doing this type of activity. I believe them because they have lined the beach pointing and clapping as I ride my Wah-Wah board across the waves just north of the river mouth. The fishermen heading out to sea in their colorful cubic painted boats quietly stare as I ride the left barrels that break for a good sixty yards or more. Several of the more adventurous kids grab pieces of wood washed up on the shore and join me in the water: The first boogie boarders in Harper.

Just south of this particular point, on the backside of the harbor, I spied a right break from the cliffs above. I paddled out of a small cove lying at the bottom of the cliffs until I reached the reef. The water is dark blue, very much in contrast to the murky water at the river mouth. Although the ride isn't very long, about twenty yards at most, it's a fun spot and easy to surf as it breaks out in open water. The Wah-Wah board handles surprising well and I am able to make basic cuts and turns, and walk the nose. I am surfing this lonesome reef break one afternoon when a local fishermen paddles up to me in his dug out canoe and points to the water below. I have no idea what he is trying to tell me until he reaches down into the dug out canoe and shows me. He pulls up a seven-foot hammerhead by its anvil shaped snout, holding the deadly creature between his locked elbows and forearms. He drops the shark back into his canoe, shaking his head back and forth as he slowly paddles away. I continue surfing. What else am I going to do, not surf, thus proving the cat from Pennsylvania right?

At this point I've lost my complacency, especially when I'm paddling to or from this particular break, or whenever I lose my Wah-Wah board and have to chase it down. Just yesterday, as I was making my way out at the river mouth, I felt a sharp pain suddenly shoot up my leg. I quickly jumped on my Wah-Wah board, my heart racing with fear, franticly looking about for torn flesh, blood and fins. I'd merely stepped on a ray. Surfing completely alone in these waters, I am continually thinking about that fisherman and his catch.

The motorbike the U.N. has loaned me really comes in handy as I can now travel along the coast with my eight-six Wah-Wah board. I merely shove the nose of the Wah-Wah board up against the gas tank, resting the remaining length of board across the seat and rear rack. Then I sit on the board and cruise the coast, occasionally taking a girlfriend. There aren't many places to surf in this area of Liberia and the waters are extremely dangerous. Most of the coastline is just a straight beach and when wading into the water, I might get ten feet from the water's edge before it suddenly drops straight off, quickly finding myself in water twenty feet deep or more: Great hunting grounds for the sharks in the area. I've sat many afternoons underneath coconut trees with a girlfriend rubbing my monkey belly watching fins patrolling the shore. This unique shelf structure is also ripe for creating powerful undertows. Drowning in Liberia is a very common fate.

When my time with the Peace Corps was over, I decided it was prudent of me to leave my Wah-Wah board behind, but I don't think anyone has used it since.

And to this day, I can still hear the drums and that cat's

voice from Pennsylvania: "No-one can surf here."

Grand Pa

The black and white photo was faded but in good shape for having survived this long in the tropics. The man standing in the center was thick with muscles, his body stood taunt and strong. Only his eyes were smiling.

None of this surprises me; whenever I'm allowed to snap a photograph, practically everyone stands this way, hiding their relaxed nature, yet exposing their intense respect. Grandma, though, adamantly refuses to have her picture taken; she believes the camera can steal her soul. Grandpa has no such fears.

"A Catholic Priest took this photo, one of the few pictures of the people he took here. He was, on many levels, a frustrated man." A sly proud smile covers Nyanti's face.

The photo reminds me of my own Papa who started his working life in the coal mines of Kansas at the age of nine years old. I see the resemblance in Nyanti and his father.

"I have a good size home", Nyanti explains, "The custom is that a man can have as much land as he can keep brushed and cleaned. Our land stretches just over to that hill and down there towards the creek."

I am very impressed because the jungle grows rapidly here. Nyanti is constantly swinging his cutlass, cutting the grass to maintain his own, and that of his father. Nyanti is also the principal at the local Catholic school- a school without a priest or a nun, a school run entirely by Nyanti and donations, a Catholic school buried deep in JuJu territory.

The people are very open here, yet they keep secrets, leery of being called a Big Shot. Just as Nyanti is careful not to boast too much, or to let others know how much rent I pay, he is also careful to share: but not like a Big Shot.

"The Almond tree, planted here, the one you sit under, my father planted this tree the day when his first child was born." I already knew Charles was the first born child.

"How many children did your father have?"

"Seven."

"Where are they? I only know you."

"Several died, several left. Some to Monrovia and some further." I notice a subtle change in Nyanti's appearance. Nyanti is an educated man, having been educated by Franciscan's brave enough to live an entire life in the middle of nowhere and for no money. I wait for his answer.

"I have always had a dream, to see the World before I died."

I ask him a stupid question, "Why don't you go?"

Nyanti holds the photograph in his hands, gently rubbing the edges. "Life is hard in the jungle; my mother and my father need me."

I am learning that the more life changes, and the more places I visit, the more it remains the same. I notice grandpa moving around the outskirts of the house. He seems lost. Nyanti answers my question without me having to sound ignorant.

"My father is starving himself to death. He doesn't want to live any more. Arthritis has left him crippled; he has no use of his hands and he has decided he has no more use here." Nyanti rubs the photograph again.

I am normally awakened by the rooster's first call; today, I am awakened by a loud knock on the door. Darkness continues to fill the room as I reach for a candle to light my way. I quietly call out, "Who's there?" I wait for the usual reply of "Dat Me".

There is only silence. Then, another knock.

"Who Dare?" I wait for the other common response, "I'd Da One, I'd Da One." Nothing but a single knock: I open the door.

Grandpa is standing in the doorway, his hands and face clasped in knots. His eyes, however, aren't. They hold something much more.

Grandpa and I have never talked, I assume it's because he doesn't speak English, few people here do, and I have yet to learn Kru, except for a few words of greeting and goodbye. I am not sure that the Kru language has ever been written down, at least no one here has offered me a written version; it's a language of sound and my ears aren't that sharp. I tell him hello: Anewtay. I step aside for him to come in. He points towards the farm. It's early and I'm confused. I walk to the kitchen and bring back a jar of coffee; he shakes his head in agreement. Starting up the Kerosene stove, I offer him a banana, he refuses.

Pouring boiling water into the cup of dried coffee, I pick up a can of condensed milk; he slowly raises and lowers both eyebrows. Silence can be awkward, but I never find that to be so here. Grandpa cups the coffee in his clubbed hands. His eyes scan the room while brushing his bare feet on the concrete floor: the concrete floor Charles and Mr. Weah have placed down, concrete bought from the rent I pay. I watch him slowly raise his gaze to the wooden shutters covering the windows, tracing them as he glances at the new tin roof: his eyes betray his face.

Grandpa never paid much attention to me; he had more important things on his mind than another Kupee venturing into the jungle, into his home. I hear the first rooster's call; grandpa finishes his coffee.

Silence is an interesting aspect of language, many times, words never need to be spoken, and many times, words should never be spoken. Grandpa never ventured over to Nyanti's new house after that day, he had more important things on his mind.

My last day in the village, as I slowly pack and get myself ready to leave, I hear a gentle knock on the open door. I casually raise and lower both eyebrows. Grandma quietly approaches, touching both me and my camera: I can see Grandpa walking the fringes of the property they own where Charles has recently planted a small palm tree orchard from the palms I retrieved from a distant commercial farm. Grandma stands as they almost always do, when you take their picture.

EPILOGUE

GBOYO

The whole country has descended into madness. There seems to be no sanity left- the Gboyos have taken over. They were always here and will probably always be here, but now the country is run amuck with them. The sole quest for power and wealth has created the chaos of a relentless civil war, engulfing the entire region. Caba had been right, hopefully, Nyanti was right too.

Charles Taylor, Alhaj Kromah, Prince Johnson, Foday Sankoh and those like them have turned Liberia and its neighbors into a living hell. They have turned boys and girls, as young as seven years old, into killing machines, filling and polluting their minds with dope and JuJu. Officials estimate that 18,000 children, seventeen years old and younger, are now ex-soldiers of that war. Close to two thirds of the Liberian population were witnesses to murder, rape, mutilation or torture, and out of those eyewitnesses, seventy-seven percent where related to the victims.

Ten percent of the population was murdered while three-quarters of the population were either displaced or are refugees. Of the 60,000 rebels, sixty percent were children but those who suffered most were the women. Even today, they can't come up with an accurate count of how many women were raped because it's too large. Not only were they raped, they were gang raped, and they were raped on multiple occasions. They were raped in front of their children, their friends, their fathers and their mothers. Many women and children were literally raped to death. They were raped while their husbands were forced to watch, and when the perpetrators of these horrendous acts were finished, they'd chop off the husband's heads, forcing the raped women to watch. Pregnant women were hunted down by these doped up sadistic scoundrels just so they could cut them open and bet on whether the unborn was a boy or a girl, leaving them there to die and rot on the side of the road. Meanwhile, the world stood by and did nothing. Why did the world turn a blind eye to all of this?

Who are these Gboyos who seem so perversely excited by all their crimes, and where do they exist? They exist everywhere, not just in the jungles of West

Africa. They are the ones who are robbing and sacrificing others out of their own desire to acquire more power or to hang on to the power they presently have. They all spew high and mighty words, rationalizing their killings with all kinds of righteous testaments and praises of God and patriotism. Their ranks include the politician, the businessman, the preacher and all their spokespersons.

Many of them are highly educated, like Francis Nyepan, who held a Masters degree in education from Harvard University in the United States. He was a member of the gang of twelve who were accused, convicted and hung for the kidnapping and brutal ritualistic killing of Moses Tweh, a popular singer and fisherman from Maryland County. But the Gboyos and their members, in my minds eye, includes not only the people who commit these ritualistic killings but also includes anyone who condones these murders and any other atrocities associated with their acts, it includes anyone who blatantly ignores them, or in anyway, directly or indirectly, supports them. In my humble opinion, an honorary member in this society is one Mr. James Pinkerton, the famous columnist for the far right.

In a Newsday article titled "Who are we to decide Liberia's civil war," published on July 29, 2003, well after all the above facts were known, and after all the horrors of Rwanda were exposed, he wrote that the United States shouldn't interfere with Liberia because it wasn't worth losing any of our soldiers over. He compared this brutal civil war in Liberia to our own Civil War. He wrote, " If the bleeding European liberals had interfered then, America wouldn't be what it is today." He argued that the United States should just let them fight it out, letting the cards fall as they may. His written statement of "just let them fight it out" not only condones the terrorizing, murdering and raping of tens of thousands of innocent civilians trapped there, but willfully encourages such savage acts. There is absolutely no way anyone could, or should, reasonably compare our Civil War with what is occurring in West Africa today. That's unless, of course, they are part of the Gboyo society.

This is what I am talking about. When a highly educated and influential man takes a cold, callous and indifferent stance to genocide, mass murder, mutilation and rape, when that man publishes an article that is cold, callous and indifferent to war crimes being committed over a fourteen-year period, and even longer when you take West Africa as a whole, that person deserves an honorary membership into the Gboyo society. Why did he take such a stance? Is it because it isn't financially beneficial to intervene? If you were witnessing similar acts in your own backyard what would you do, call your accountant? Well, in today's ever shrinking world, Africa is our back yard. These gangsters, mobsters and murderers afforded their wars by selling millions of dollars worth of diamonds on the black market, one of whose buyers included Al Queda. The CIA estimated Al Queda purchased over $10 million dollars worth of diamonds from Charles Taylor, thus fueling their rampage.

Yet it wouldn't be fair of me not to include others in this honorary brotherhood of Gboyos. What of President Bill Clinton, who idly sat by as a million or more Rwandans experienced a similar fate? Or Jesse Jackson and his support for Charles Taylor and Fonday Sankoh which has led Mr. Jackson to be known in Africa as the "killer rights" leader. What of the Bush administration who so actively courts the black vote but does nothing about the situation in West Africa: or Katrina? And what of the other commentators of the far right ideology who continually scream for law and order, who shout over the airwaves 24/7 that justice needs to be done as they wail about the softhearted bleeding liberals being soft on crime and terrorism. My question is, "Exactly, where are the police? Why don't they intervene and stop these horrendous crimes from being committed, and why are these outraged blow-hard conservatives turning a blind eye to a problem that is of such a huge magnitude that the repercussions will be felt for generations to come?" But to Pinkerton and his likes, it just isn't worth the trouble. In fact, the only real international police force we have they continually ridicule and demean, working constantly to undermine and dismantle these forces. Why do you suppose that is?

And then there is Pat Robertson himself, the vanguard of Christian ethics and values, who has invested millions and has signed contracts not only with Charles Taylor for gold mining rights in the Bukon Jedeh region of Liberia, but also signed a diamond mining contract with the ex-dictator of Zaire, Mobu Sese Seko, who, when he was still alive, also had business dealings with terrorists organizations. And Charles Taylor, besides having business dealings with Pat Robertson, also had extensive business relationships with renowned criminals such as Ibrahim Bah, a Libyan trained Senegalese terrorist who fought in Afghanistan in the eighties and joined Hezbollah in the nineties; Victor Bout, the largest illegal weapons merchant in the world; Leonid Menin, Ukrainian drug lord; Plus a variety of South African and Balkan criminal organizations. If the United States was serious about the Patriot Act and its goals, then Pat Robertson should be arrested and tried on terrorist and treason charges for having directly or indirectly, knowingly or unknowingly, provided either material or moral support to the terrorists, especially Al Qaeda, who have been able to launder millions in cash by buying diamonds which are easily smuggled and exchanged. Why is Pat Robertson doing business with such a person as Charles Taylor?

Yes, the Gboyos are everywhere, and I ask myself, is there a difference from kidnapping someone and mutilating them to attain personal power, or from strapping a bomb to one's self to drive out the infidels in order to obtain martyrdom, or from bombing people from 30,000 feet with the sole intention of securing ones own demand for oil and economic growth, or from driving down the street shooting a pistol from a car window for the sole personal glory of being a gangster? All these people are Gboyos and everyone who supports them is a part of their Gboyo society. Now I am left with the question of, "Why exactly do we wage war and to whose rescue do we come to?"

I wholeheartedly support capitalism and the United States Constitution. I am a firm believer in Adam Smith and the principles of our Founding

Fathers. I think the Declaration of Independence is one of the greatest documents ever written. Some of the most powerful words are contained in the very first sentence of the Declaration of Independence: "It is the inalienable right of all men to life, liberty and the pursuit of happiness." It sorrows me to no end when I hear people talk the talk but don't walk the walk. It's even more tragic when people who claim to be an American, fail, or refuse, to talk the talk, or in this case, write it, especially when confronted with the enormity of the human disaster currently taking place in West Africa: and it's even worse, when they financially back our enemies out of selfish greed.

Right now the entire World seems perched on the edge of chaos and doom, yet so far, we have survived. Why is that? And if we are to continue to survive, what can we do about it? I have no answer, but we have witnessed throughout our human history actions of many prophets, leaders and individuals who have demonstrated what can be achieved with courage, strength, wisdom and love.

West Africa has a tremendous amount of wealth in its soil, ranging from diamonds and gold, to timber and oil; it is also the home of a great number of powerful souls. And like all souls, we are all exactly one of the same; with each one of us being different and unique onto ourselves. Now is not the time to bury our heads in the sand and continue thinking in our old dogmatic ways. Everywhere you turn there is a war going on, and the soldiers in these wars, and the victims in these wars, are woman and children. Do we do as the Pinkertons ask us to do: to ignore their plight and let them be brutally sacrificed so we can hang onto the power we presently have? Do we act as the Robertsons have behaved and invest in the continuance of this human carnage, hoping only to enrich ourselves? Or do we mobilize ourselves as we did in World War II and confront and defeat these Gboyos?

Has the whole world descended into madness? Have the Gboyos taken over? They were always here and probably always will be, but now the world seem to be run amuck with them. The sole quest for power and wealth has created the chaos of relentless civil wars engulfing the entire planet. The question now is: "Where do we go from here?"

The battle between good and evil is a battle that has been waged every single day ever since the beginning of time primordial. Back in the 1920s Herbert Hoover, the President of the United States, pointed it out for us when he said "Instead of the glorification of the cowardly gangsters, we need to the glorification of policemen who do their duty and give their lives in public protection. If the police had vigilant, universal backing of public opinion in their communities, if they had the implacable support of the prosecuting authorities and the courts, I am convinced that our police would stamp out the excessive crime which has disgraced some of our great cities."

I've been told that the greatest enlightenment is selfish enlightenment, roughly meaning: All boats rise with a rising tide, and all boats fall with an outgoing tide. I've also been told that if you want to know what the future holds, just look at what's in your hands. Now, ask yourself, "Who are we to decide Liberia's civil war?" As far as I am concerned, J.P. Gboyo might as well have titled his article, "Who are we to decide or do anything?" He should have published his cold, callous, ignorant and irresponsible article in the Daily Gboyo Times. "Pat Gboyo Robertson" shouldn't be calling his mining company "The Freedom Mining Co."; He should be calling it "The Gboyo Mining Co."

It's time for all of us to ask ourselves what is important in this life? More importantly, it's time for all of us to stop sacrificing others just so we can attain more power and wealth. It's time we opened our eyes, our ears and our minds; it's time we quit acting like we've just fallen out of the trees and put clothes on our back. It's time to Bless up.

DANTE'S GATE

When I become
Greater than you
My thoughts and ideas
To be weighted
Heavier than yours
And my hunger
More important than yours
Then war has begun
When I ascend
So my God
Is the only God
Allowing me vengeance
And the righteousness of truth
Then war has begun
When claiming lands as mine
Those you once roamed
Dictating to you
Commanding you
Then war has begun
When I see not you
In me
And me
Not in you
And sharing is the sin
Then war has begun
When atrocities

Affect me no more
And the slaughtering
The raping and the mutilation
Of my fellow human being
Causes me to turn a blind eye
Then the end has begun